D1388939

# ADRENALIZED

www.transworldbooks.co.uk

# ADRENALIZED
## LIFE, *DEF LEPPARD* AND BEYOND

### PHIL COLLEN

#### WITH CHRIS EPTING

## BANTAM PRESS

LONDON  •  TORONTO  •  SYDNEY  •  AUCKLAND  •  JOHANNESBURG

TRANSWORLD PUBLISHERS
61–63 Uxbridge Road, London W5 5SA
www.transworldbooks.co.uk

Transworld is part of the Penguin Random House group of companies
whose addresses can be found at global.penguinrandomhouse.com

Penguin
Random House
UK

First published in Great Britain in 2015 by Bantam Press
an imprint of Transworld Publishers

A CIP catalogue record for this book
is available from the British Library.

ISBN 9780593073193 (hb)
9780593073209 (tpb)

Typeset in 12¾/17¼pt Adobe Garamond by Falcon Oast Graphic Art Ltd.
Printed and bound by Clays Ltd, Bungay, Suffolk.

Penguin Random House is committed to a sustainable
future for our business, our readers and our planet. This book
is made from Forest Stewardship Council® certified paper.

MIX
Paper from
responsible sources
FSC® C018179

1 3 5 7 9 10 8 6 4 2

For my dad, Ken, and my mum, Connie

# 1

I came into this world on 8 December 1957, in Hackney, a London borough located in East London. A day or so after being born at the Mothers' Hospital of the Salvation Army on Lower Clapton Road, I was brought home to 223 Boundary Road, London, where I would spend a large chunk of my life until 1983, when I went on tour with Def Leppard. It was a small row house in a working-class neighbourhood that was considered to be pretty rough. It didn't seem like that at the time because I had nothing to compare it to. My dad, Ken Collen, was actually born in Wales, even though he grew up in East London. He was a lorry driver (or a trucker, as they're known in the States) his entire life. He loved driving, so even when he wasn't working, it wasn't a chore for him to drive us all over the place. We'd call it a 'busman's holiday'. That's an old British phrase that describes a vacation on which you still do the same kind of activity you'd normally do in your job. My mum, Connie Collen (née Wheeler), was from nearby Leytonstone. She became a housewife as soon as I was born, and we spent lots of time together while my dad was off on his frequent driving trips for work. I was the only child they'd ever have. As far as my mum was concerned, the sun rose and fell on my arse. My grandmother, my mum's mother – Nan, as I called her – stayed with us because my mum needed a bit more help. My mum's two older sisters, Dorothy and Rosie, were really strong women. (My wife, Helen, and I recently went to visit my auntie Dorothy. She was ninety-two, vegetarian and doing great.) My mum was weaker physically, suffering from a variety of ailments, including asthma (which I think I psychologically inherited from her) and scarlet fever. So my nan was there to lend a hand even after my mum got married.

All of East London was very working class – Hackney, Walthamstow, Leyton and Leytonstone. Our small house and these surrounding neighbourhoods became my universe as a youngster. I had a paper round, like a lot of other kids, so each day I would set off on foot around the neighbourhood delivering a variety of different papers to dozens of families.

Early on, I lived what I think was probably a very similar experience for lots of other English kids of that period. I had a dog, Coffee, who was a Jack Russell–beagle mix. I was about four or five years when I got Coffee. I was always so paranoid that he'd run out the door and get hit by a car. This compounded the asthma. As a kid in school I played a lot of football (or soccer) like everyone else, and we played in the huge area of grassland on the western bank of the River Lea called the Hackney Marshes. In fact, Hackney Marshes is where my dad first took my training wheels off my bike. The place was later to become a part of the 2012 Olympic stadium. Talk about expanding your universe. The West Ham (my team), Arsenal and Tottenham teams were all within striking distance, and all the kids supported one of those. Leyton Orient, another football club, was walking distance from my house, but no one supported them because the poor fuckers were in the Third Division. My dream – like that of all British kids – was to play professional football.

One of my fondest memories of growing up is of the weekends and holidays that we would take to Southend, Jaywick, Clacton-on-Sea or Canvey Island, places at the end of the Thames Estuary, where the Thames filters into the North Sea. Even though these places were barely an hour away from home, people of limited means could escape there from the city and feel as though they had entered some exotic playground. I've read recently that Jaywick is today considered one of the most deprived areas in the country, but at the time, those trips represented adventure, escapism and my love of travel.

My parents smoked like troopers. They were completely

unaware of the hideous side effects this would have on their sickly child and how it was probably making my asthma worse. Swimming was suggested by my doctor to relieve my asthma because he refused to place me on an inhaler for fear of me becoming reliant on the drugs. I loved to swim and was swimming about a mile by the time I was eight years old. I actually became a fairly decent swimmer and diver, and joined several swim teams while I was in school.

As I was growing up, my parents taught me (like many other post-Second World War kids) to appreciate what you have and not to harp on about what you don't have. They were very frugal and I know a lot of that stems from the lean years they spent during the war in England. That mentality seeped everywhere, even down to what we ate. As with most families at the time, our diet wasn't quite what I would call healthy, but, then again, we managed to survive on British sustenance. That is to say, lots of braised beef, along with plenty of mashed and boiled potatoes. Then of course there was also what we Brits called pork scratchings or pork cracklings (also known as pork rinds), which were just basically fried and roasted pork fat; another pig delicacy was dripping, which was congealed fat spread on a slice of bread. So once again, I had nothing to compare all of this to until I had my first curry.

I would have conversations with my mum, sitting in our small kitchen while she peeled potatoes for dinner. I would sit there quietly as she told me stories about the war with a certain love and pride in her voice even as she recounted in great detail what it was like to be a child and live through the Blitz in 1940 and 1941, when the Germans launched massive and sustained strategic bombings all across the United Kingdom, when more than one million London houses were destroyed or damaged and more than 40,000 civilians were killed. My mum and her family would hop from bomb shelter to bomb shelter throughout her neighbourhood, and by forces of both luck and common sense they managed to survive.

As the adage goes, what didn't kill everyone made them stronger, and my parents were living proof of that, as were many other people in our neighbourhood. My mum always stressed to me how the war and severe rationing made people pull together and how proud she was of her country's ironclad patriotism. To this day, this is a big part of who I am. I will always go around my house looking for lights and/or water to turn off and such, due to the fact that both of my parents instilled in me this sense of never wasting anything. When you grow up taking one bath a week to conserve water and rationing your meals because you never knew when things could be taken away from you, it reminds you that it's always a good idea to conserve and not take anything for granted.

One of my closest friends, Gary Saint, lived in the next street over. I'd known Gary since we were about eight years old. He'd be at my house all the time. He'd even come on my parents' weekend trips to Jaywick and remained a loyal friend well into our adult lives together. There was a group of us that hung out together, like kids do. I remember it being a wonderful childhood where members of our little gang were within shouting distance of each other's houses.

To anyone passing by, Boundary Road and the surrounding area looked like the countless other grey and dreary English cityscapes. But it was a thriving, colourful place, inhabited and enhanced by people of many cultures. We all lived alongside many immigrants from the Indian subcontinent and the Caribbean, including a huge influx of Jamaicans, who brought with them the sound of reggae, which would influence many musicians in the 1960s. As I walked home from school each day, the air was thick with the aromas of many different and wild-smelling foods. All the various kinds of pungent curries and spices, fresh ginger, and those mouthwatering, aromatic smells gave our neighbourhood a rich, ethnic flavour (both figuratively and literally). That is not to say we didn't have our fair share of racism on our streets. Many Brits harboured deep anger toward the influx of Indians and Pakistanis, who were encouraged to come to the country for work. They called it Paki-bashing. I knew kids who were singled out and attacked simply because they were Indian or Pakistani. I never understood it.

Being around people of different ethnic groups was

nothing new to me. My mum's oldest sister, my auntie Dorothy, had three daughters – my first cousins. They were all married to black men. So a part of my family is multi-racial. To me it was strange to see the separatism of races pushed by propaganda. Nothing new there. It was no surprise that white-bread Britain, with its strong Anglo-Saxon foundation, would have a problem with the newly integrated brown population.

By the early 1960s, when I was just seven or eight years old, I started listening to the radio as if it were this great and brilliant discovery. It was the radio that opened a whole new world, and that world was named the Beatles. I became obsessed with Paul, John, Ringo and George, pretty much like every other kid with a pulse back then. I loved their songs, how the guys looked, everything. I remember that thrill of sitting in our front room waiting for any song by the Fab Four to come on the radio. As soon as it did, my friend Terry from next door and I would go to the shed (aka 'the stage') behind my house and pretend that we were John Lennon and Paul McCartney, substituting tennis rackets for guitars and donning plastic Beatle wigs that were popular then. Often to the annoyance of our neighbours, we'd cry out our own strangled versions of 'I Want to Hold Your Hand' and 'Twist and Shout'.

The mid-1960s were absolutely mind-blowing in terms of what one could find on the radio, and not just the Beatles. And not just on the BBC, which actually had a fairly limited selection of music. No, to find what was really going on, we tuned in to underground broadcasting outlets. There was Radio Luxembourg and pirate radio stations that offered some remarkable sonic lifelines from America, including artists like the Beach Boys, Aretha Franklin, Stevie Wonder, and all of the big Motown artists of the day. Pirate radio was broadcasted illegally, without a licence, by ships anchored miles off the coast of England. Radio Caroline, Wonderful Radio London, Swinging Radio England – these fantastically mysterious stations kept us all completely plugged into music that was part of the 'Swinging London' scene that had begun to flourish in the mid-1960s. You had the British Invasion, which included the Beatles, Stones, Kinks, the Who and the Small Faces. You had psychedelic rock from Jimi Hendrix (I'm claiming Hendrix because he broke in England first) to Cream and Pink Floyd and others. And you had mod fashions and sexy pop tarts like Jean Shrimpton, Penelope Tree and Twiggy. All of these converged in London Town in one huge, swirling orgy of culture, fashion, and especially music.

It was in this atmosphere that you felt something important was shifting. One day you would hear 'Like a Rolling Stone' for the very first time. Then you might hear 'Satisfaction', or 'My Generation'. It was the 1959 Colin MacInnes novel about London, *Absolute Beginners*, brought to life. The ground was shaking. There was something charged and intoxicating in the air. London seemed to be the centre of it. Living in Walthamstow, and with it being a suburb, we did not have direct contact with all the glittery, seductive charms of Swinging London, but it did trickle down to us in the way of music. I had a partner in crime who explored this new amazing world with me, my cousin Dave Wheeler.

It's hard to measure the influence Dave had on me. He was two years older than me, so it was a bit like having an older brother. Being an only child, I never had that sort of older sibling to influence me, shape me, or even to corrupt me musically. But thankfully Dave did all those things. Dave was my mum's oldest brother Georgie's son and he lived in one of three tower blocks just paces off Boundary Road. This was our social centre. We played football, went out with girls, and just got up to no good in general. Dave and I actually went out with two sisters who were two years apart. My girl's name was Kim Taylor. She was dark-haired and I considered her to be my first girlfriend. Dave was going out with her older sister, Pat. But even more important than that, Dave exposed me to a wild, all-you-could-eat musical buffet that affects me to this very day – he was an amazing connoisseur of music, especially guitar-driven rock. But he wasn't just a big fan of music – he also had access to rare and wonderful under-the-counter bootleg albums back then, trawling vinyl shops throughout London's East End to procure some of the finest illegal concert recordings known to man. These vinyl treasures announced themselves differently than regular albums. Forget the slick packaging. We're talking a plain white cardboard sleeve, usually with a colour-mimeographed piece of cover art scotch-taped on the front. They looked and felt like contraband – sonic taboo – and Dave treasured his hot wax. I always preferred the real recordings, but the artists that he exposed me to were the real magic – Hendrix, Zeppelin, the Stones, Floyd and of course Deep Purple, all of which he blasted out of his stereo. A bunch of us would go up to his mum and dad's flat and greedily absorb it all.

When I was about fourteen years old, I had an epiphany. I remember seeing David Bowie and the Spiders from Mars on *Top of the Pops*. They were playing this type of music that just spoke to me. It seemed that Bowie was directly writing songs for my group of friends. I had never heard or seen anything like Bowie in my life. It was all brand new – totally androgynous. Since I was a sponge, it was ultimately cool. Although Bowie spearheaded the glam rock movement, along with Marc Bolan of T. Rex, the real hook was the amazing songs and melodies that Bowie wrote. Then there was the fact that he obviously didn't give a fuck about how people perceived the way he looked, even though it was a very contrived concept. When I first saw Little Richard, I was too young to know that he was effeminate. But when I saw Bowie, he overdid the androgyny and was wearing glitter, coloured hair and girls' clothes. It was certainly nothing anyone in England had seen before. As a teenager trying to discover myself, I thought that this seemed like a gang I could belong to. Then there was the amazing look and playing of his guitarist, Mick Ronson, which totally hooked me.

When I later saw David Bowie and the Spiders from Mars on *The Old Grey Whistle Test*, it further sealed the deal for me. *The Old Grey Whistle Test* was a music television show that ran on BBC Two, and I'm sure that, besides me, it influenced many other kids of my generation. The beauty of *The Old Grey Whistle Test* was that it was all very low-key. Bands would perform their songs in a very plain-looking studio without lots of production, which forced you to really focus on the music. There was no studio audience, so you could practically hear a pin drop between songs. To this day I love looking up clips from the show on YouTube. It's sort of like time stands still. As soon as I hear the opening title music – a cool, groovy harmonica-based song called 'Stone Fox Chase' by the Nashville band called Area Code 615, I'm back to being that wide-eyed boy in the living room. The sound of that opening was just so rootsy. You knew you were going to get an untarnished view of whatever artists happened to be on the programme that week. The show's original host when it started back in 1971 was Richard Williams, but on this magical night in 1972, the laid-back 'Whispering' Bob Harris (as he was known) by then had taken the helm. The programme took its strange name from an old Tin Pan Alley phrase. According to legend, agents would have the doormen for the building come in and listen to a song and see if it was worthwhile – the 'test' was whether the 'old grey' folks could whistle the tune.

All I remember is Bowie playing an acoustic guitar and Mick Ronson playing his famous Les Paul, banging out 'Queen Bitch'. The interesting thing was that as different and new as his image was, he didn't look like some dude wearing make-up. He looked like David Bowie. The whole visual thing Bowie gave off combined with his expression of the music made him seem like part of some exclusive club I desperately wanted to belong to. Of course Bowie was speaking to me. The first line of 'Queen Bitch' was, 'I'm up on the eleventh floor and I'm watching the cruisers below . . .' and Dave's family lived on the eleventh floor.

*The Old Grey Whistle Test*, by the way, would go on to host lots of other legendary performances as I got older. It's where Bob Marley and the Wailers made their very first British TV appearance. I also remember seeing Stevie Marriott and Humble Pie and Bill Withers, amongst many other legendary performers, not to mention, later, a performance by a band called Girl, of which I would soon become a member. But of all of the artists that I saw on the *Whistle Test* no one dazzled, dazed and amazed me the way David Bowie did. Thanks to him, in one single moment, my world went from black-and-white to colour.

If seeing Bowie on television was a landmark moment for me, then so was the day that Dave and I went to our first live rock concert. Neither one of us had ever seen a live show, so this was a big deal. We went to see Deep Purple, who in 1972 were one of my favourite bands. They were out on the road for their *Machine Head* tour, and they were playing at the Sundown Brixton (now known as O2 Academy Brixton), a former movie house that dated back to 1929. It was (and still is) a classic-looking theatre, held about 3,000 or so and was built to feel like an amphitheatre set in an Italian garden. It had just been refurbished for concerts and this night, 30 September, was actually to be the very first rock-and-roll show held at the venue. A christening of sorts, in more ways than one, and we were going to be there to experience it.

I don't remember queuing up, but we stumbled in and were front row propping up the stage. We were totally excited. Even the opening act, Glencoe (crap name, crap band), freaked me out because I had never seen a live band before. So when drummer Ian Paice, bassist Roger Glover, singer Ian Gillan, keyboardist Jon Lord, and especially lead guitarist Ritchie Blackmore strolled onstage, it honestly left me breathless. Ritchie Blackmore stood right in front of me. It was surreal. I think people tend to forget that in the pre-MTV world rock stars truly were godlike, mythical figures of lore that were quite different than mere mortals. There they were, just as they appeared on the album covers and in the magazines. Flesh and blood. Deep Purple. I was just trying to take it all in.

From the opening number, 'Highway Star', I was completely mesmerized. They played everything. 'Smoke on the Water', 'Space Truckin'' and more. It was loud, thunderous and energizing. Pushed up front against the wooden stage I could see, feel, hear and practically taste each note as it was played. What I saw Ritchie Blackmore do that night – the range of styles he displayed – was stupefying. He played classical, jazz, blues, rock and roll – he just blew me away. As I reached up toward him, he slapped my hand.

At the end of the show, as they plowed through the encore, 'Lucille', Blackmore smashed his Fender Strat on the stage. I was euphoric. Actually, sitting here now thinking about that night, words can't really describe how I felt. I may have left my body. *Oh my God*, I thought. *That's what I want to do! I want to be that guy up there!*

Many professional musicians will reflect upon a specific time when they saw their future, their destiny, their fate, whatever you want to call it, all converge in one spectacular and explosive moment. This was mine. Ironically, it wasn't until many years later when Def Leppard played the Brixton Academy that I realized it was the same building as the former Sundown and that the reason I played guitar on that side of the stage was because that was where Blackmore had played. It was actually really freaky looking out on the audience and remembering that this was the first place I had ever been to a show. Then there I was, on the same stage, looking out at the audience. Years after attending my first show, I was looking at *Made in Japan* – a live Deep Purple album recorded in Japan – and I said to myself, *Hey, these fans don't look Japanese!* referring to the audience members. Upon further inspection, to my joy, I saw me!! There I was, front row, propping up the stage at my very first concert.

The intensity and creativity that Ritchie displayed that night completely convinced me that I had to go home and persuade my mum and dad that they needed to buy me an electric guitar. But guitars were expensive, and it would take two years of pestering.

So I began my pestering routine for an electric guitar. I didn't know my parents would go into debt to get me this guitar. Although when I was younger I knew it was a sacrifice, as an adult the gravity of what they did really hit home. While I waited it out, I'd go over to my pal Steve Hewer's house and play air guitar pretending to be Bowie, Slade and T. Rex. Steve showed me my first barre chord and taught me how to play songs like Hawkwind's 'Silver Machine' on his guitar.

I also filled my time seeing more shows: the beauty of living in London was that everybody played there. So I got to witness a plethora of amazing bands, especially – and finally – David Bowie on his *Aladdin Sane* tour at Earls

Court in London on 12 May 1973. I vividly remember my mum and dad dropping me and Martin Blackman off at the venue. The whole night – from how the audience dressed to Bowie and the Spiders onstage – was a spectacle. Even though I think Martin and me were the only two out of 18,000 fans that didn't dress up in some crazy outfit, it was strange to be part of the alienesque Bowie tribe. His fans were so obsessively dedicated to looking like him, dressing like him and adopting his persona that it was as if we were within the colourful bowels of some glittery cult. But we loved it. We felt special and anointed. And when he finally hit the stage I almost couldn't believe it was really him. In the flesh!

Bowie at this point was at his creative peak. The make-up, the glam, the glitter, the killer songs were dazzling, with Broadway-like precision and energy. But as captivating as Bowie was, it was his guitar player, Mick Ronson, who all but stole the show. It was amazing to me how he could stand out as he did without ever upstaging Bowie. There was this ultimate confidence just oozing off the stage, yet he still remained a team player. He knew how to be seen without being over-the-top. So many musicians fail to master that art.

I also saw Mott the Hoople at Hammersmith Odeon, along with then up-and-coming supporting band Queen, who blew the lid off the place. Another killer show was Led Zeppelin at Earls Court. From what I remember, when I first went inside, it sounded like some big monster had come roaring into the arena. I couldn't even tell what they were playing at first, but then it hit me: it was 'Rock and Roll', from their fourth album. Now, Earls Court is a horrible toilet. Its massive sound just bounces off really high ceilings and walls. But, back then, these shows were pure magic.

I was in awe watching the masters play their electric guitars. I loved the really flashy playing of Ronson and Blackmore, but I never thought I'd be able to play like that. To me they were superhuman. I wouldn't even know where to start. I would go to this place in the West End of London called the Fender Sound House, and sit and stare at the Fender Stratocasters and Gibson Les Pauls hanging on the walls. I would literally be drooling. Those sparkly blues, reds and purples. And the sunburst-coloured wood grains. They looked delicious to me. In quite a pervy sort of way I would touch the guitars. This was a big deal because 1) I couldn't play and 2) you weren't supposed to touch the merchandise, as the militant shopkeepers were always keeping watch. I felt that if I were to pick up one of the guitars I'd be pummelled to the ground by one of the staff. This made the guitars all the more desirable.

And then came that monumental day: my sixteenth birthday, 8 December 1973. The day I got my first guitar – a red Gibson SG. My life was about to change. This instrument represented what I dreamed would be my future. (Seriously, I would put the guitar against the wall and stare at it until I nodded off to sleep.) But as my parents told me, nobody was going to make that happen but me. True.

Along with the guitar came another birthday present – an album called *The Guitar Album*, featuring songs by both current and classic blues guitar players. Jimi Hendrix was on there, as was Duane Allman, but the tune that really jumped out at me was B. B. King's 'Sweet Sixteen'. King's playing was so sparse and intense and emotional. I felt like I could identify him after just one note, it was just that distinctive. I played his track on the record over and over, plus it was my sixteenth birthday. Ironically, in a very cool twist of fate, exactly forty years to the day, I went to see the late, great B. B. King in concert for my fifty-sixth birthday. I got to meet him. When I told him the story about my sixteenth birthday and the album I received with him singing 'Sweet Sixteen', he remarked, 'Then I should sing "Happy Birthday" to you.' And he did. (Almost a year and a half later, in 2015, he would be gone. RIP, B. B.)

Apparently, when learning how to play guitar, you're supposed to learn your chords first, which I did. But I was shocked to discover that I could play lead guitar, or solos, almost immediately. And that's really what I wanted to do. I didn't want to play 'finger-style' or 'chordal-style' backing musician. B. B. King never played chords. Like him, I wanted to be a lead guitar player straight off the bat. This was almost like being able to fly. The self-expression that I had in my head I could manifest through my fingers. Pretty fucking cool. My guitar teachers were Jimmy Page, Jimi Hendrix, Mick Ronson, Ritchie Blackmore and a host of jazz rock pioneers like Al Di Meola and Larry Coryell. Even though he was a bass player, Stanley Clarke was a big influence, too. I obviously couldn't play all of this shit they were doing, so I would take the odd phrase that really stood out to me and incorporate it into my own style. Before long I would have a collection of my favourite licks that would come to represent me. I didn't so much sit down and learn songs in their entirety – just the parts that I really loved. I did the same with singing as well. I'd just sing along to the odd line or chorus, and before you knew it, I could actually sing. This was the same thing with guitar playing. What had seemed like unattainable magic was all of a sudden within my grasp.

I had barely graduated at sixteen, and went straight to work at a burglar alarm factory. It was the first real work I had ever had, but it was the best way for me to pay back my mum for lending me three hundred quid to get my second guitar, which was a wine-red Les Paul custom. There's a picture of me playing it on the Girl album *Sheer Greed*. I didn't really know what to expect from this job. I just knew that I wasn't going to be there for long. It was a means to an end for me; otherwise it would have been really depressing. I was convinced I was going to be a rock star.

My workday started at 8 a.m. I would take a bus each morning (until I got my Honda 250 motorcycle) to the AFA burglar alarm factory, a huge building in Walthamstow. I learned a variety of different things that I never really needed to know again, except for the soldering wires part. I rotated through several departments of an assembly line, the first of which was putting screws into a plastic base. That was fairly mind-numbing. Then I was placed in the paint factory for a while, basically colouring the wires. Next I was moved into the soldering department, which I thought I had down pretty well until a few years ago, when I tried to solder a wire for one of my guitars and found that I had completely lost my soldering mojo. I knew I was colour-blind when I failed all those tests in school when you have to guess the number inside the coloured dots. But I hadn't really thought too much about it until some of these burglar alarms would fail the test – that was just me getting the coloured wires mixed up, as I'm pretty sure my soldering skills were solid back then. Pretty ironic that a colour-blind guy would be putting coloured wires into a burglar alarm. I didn't last in that department for too long. I was with AFA for only a year.

I wasn't alone – I soon found others who were also obsessed with playing and, before I knew it, we decided to form a band. And you never forget your first band. We couldn't actually play all that well, but that wasn't important at the time. I played guitar, Martin Blackman was on bass, Tony Torres did vocals, and Gary Dewing hit this drum kit that we bought for five quid.

Many houses in Britain's working-class neighbourhoods had a 'room for best'. It was for company only, and there'd be plastic over the furniture and a record player and maybe a small bar. My good friend Rudi Riviere lived in a house that was almost identical to mine, plastic covers included, but his family was from the Caribbean, so I don't know where this craze originated. My first band rehearsed at my mum's house at 223 Boundary Road in the room for best, which, thankfully, she had no problem with. We managed to get through the Hendrix version of 'Wild Thing', being that it was only three chords. In our heads, we sounded great. We did a world tour of my mum's front room. We were like a garage band with no garage. Eventually friends would come over and watch us. We also started writing our own songs, so it seemed this was as good a time as any to give ourselves a name. So I did what any naïve musician did – I closed my eyes, opened an atlas and put my finger on a page. We said wherever the finger landed, that word would be the name of the band. So our name became Moosejaw, after Moose Jaw, Saskatchewan, Canada. The name was short-lived: we disbanded after a few months over some kind of silly drama, which sort of makes you think, *Whoa! If there's drama now and we can't even play, what happens later when there is really something at stake?* I would one day find out. My first live performance would happen the very next year. I'd be seventeen years old.

London was always influential, be it in fashion or music, and had been the centre of the civilized world. It was always a hang – the Swinging Sixties; Carnaby Street, which was the fashion epicentre; and you had all of these amazing bands like the Stones, the Who, the Small Faces, the Kinks, and later Jimi Hendrix, all calling London their home. The amazing cornucopia of jazz, reggae, soul, rock, and all the cultures that music brings with it made London an encouraging and inspirational scene. The fact that you could have all of this stimuli coexisting was the reason people from all around the world flocked to this amazing city. London wasn't just the capital of England – it had been the capital of the world. Everyone would want to come there. Even the Beatles, who hailed from Liverpool, set up their own Abbey Road Studios (where Def Leppard were honoured to record a live TV show). So London really had a lot going for it. Later I was grateful to have come from such a great city – not just as a reference point, but also for the fact that you do take some of it with you wherever you go. It's an attitude/confidence thing. Then I was fairly uncultured, but after I'd travelled around the world a few times, when I went back to London I really appreciated the culture, art, architecture, etc.

But by the mid-seventies, London had gone through a

whole new transformation. The seeds had been sown in the late sixties by Iggy Pop and had later taken root in New York City, thanks to bands like the New York Dolls and the Ramones, who were responsible for a new, raw, do-it-your-self attitude, which was completely stripped down and about not giving a fuck.

The punk rock explosion in London, which kinda started in 1975 but didn't really hit the masses until the Sex Pistols appeared on Bill Grundy's *Today* programme on 1 December 1976, changed everything. It changed fashion in general, political ideals, social commentary and even how record companies operated. I don't think I ever felt as musically energized as the first time I heard the album *Never Mind the Bollocks, Here's the Sex Pistols*. To this day, that album announces itself as something radically different. It seemed pure and raw. Although everyone said these guys couldn't play, the first Pistols album had something that every rock album that had come before it couldn't get close to. It was the voice of a generation, but you had to be in England to experience it. In fact, when the Pistols album came out, all the streets were stinking due to the trash collectors going on strike because they were being taken advantage of. Their strike had nothing to do with the album, but it was all in the timing really. Everything was just fucked up. It was a time of economic depression. Unemployment was at its highest since the Second World War. State control through nationalized industries seemed to be well on the way to fulfilling George Orwell's prophesies so boldly stated in his novel *1984*. All of this rage manifested itself by kids using music as a voice because they were not being heard. With that said, it was the perfect time for a new train of thought. *Never Mind the Bollocks* was a howling buzz-saw of a record that didn't just throw down the gauntlet – it pissed and puked on it as well.

It wasn't just the Pistols' message, but the guitar was how I imagined rhythm guitar should be played in my head. The drums were how I wanted to hear them. All of this with a rather upset Johnny Rotten screaming over the top of it. Brilliant.

I could still really dig a Genesis album as well as a Pistols album. It all just broadened my horizon.

By late 1976, London was awash, with music pouring out of club after club. In addition to the Pistols, the Clash and the Damned, dozens of other musical upstarts were rebelling against the perceived pomp of bands like the Stones, Zeppelin, Floyd and the horrendous pop that was being regurgitated on the radio. This was also the era of disco, which had, like any other genre, pure genius and real shite, but was the opposite of punk. Like the mods, rockers and any counterculture groups within the same culture, it allowed kids to choose their sides.

The first live gig I ever played was with my next band, Lucy. We played for a nurses' party on Mile End Road in East London – an all-female audience. I was the youngest one onstage. I was seventeen and had moved on from burglar alarms to being a motorcycle dispatch rider for Profile Typesetting. All the other guys in the band were like twenty-three and upward. We were kinda punk without the attitude. I was scared shitless and didn't look up from my fret board all night. Even though I was petrified, once it was all over I had that first gig under my belt. I wasn't a stage virgin any more. We played mainly original songs, and I don't remember how long the set was, but I'm sure it was the longest thirty-five minutes or so of my life. At least we didn't get booed offstage. That would come later. Lucy released an EP called *You Really Got Me Going* . . . I think. After that we recorded a bunch of demos, but the real highlight for me was performing as an opening band at the Marquee Club on Wardour Street in London. The Marquee had played host to some of the most famous bands in the world. At its original location on Oxford Street, the Rolling Stones played their very first official gig in 1962. But in 1964 the club moved over to Wardour Street, where it played host to the Stones once again, the Who, Jimi Hendrix, Deep Purple, Stevie Wonder, Pink Floyd and many others. The Stones even came back to the famous club in 1971 to film a television special, and Bowie filmed *The 1980 Floor Show* there, where he famously sang the duet 'I Got You, Babe' with Marianne Faithfull dressed as a nun.

In addition to playing the Marquee, something else

happened in my life at this time. My parents got divorced. I was kind of bummed that they hadn't said anything to me prior to that and that they would do this ultra-British thing and not communicate with each other. So they drifted apart until it was unbearable for both of them. They kept it from me for the sake of not wanting to upset me. When we eventually spoke about it, I remember saying that I would have been cool if they had just mentioned it to me. I'd have said, 'Don't stay together for my sake.' What ended up happening was that my dad, being on the road so much as a lorry driver, was always gone for weeks on end, driving to Scotland, Liverpool and all over the place. So he simply grew apart from my mum, and she from him, given all the free time she had. There was no malice or any real arguments that I remember, just a gentle and obvious growing apart that resulted in both of them deciding that that was the way to go.

Divorce was still a fairly taboo subject in the mid-1970s and I didn't know a lot of other kids who came from what we call broken homes. But my home never really felt broken. I had a great life as a kid, and it remained great even in the midst of my parents' divorce, and they continued to be friends. Besides, I was eighteen at the time and cool with their decision. I certainly didn't love one parent more than the other, nor did I harbour any resentment toward either of them. I wish they had actually done it sooner.

My dad moved out soon afterward and eventually hooked

up with a woman named Doris, who was really cool. She brought my dad out of his shell and even got him to dance (which he loved doing) and to give up smoking. My mum, my nan and me carried on at home. I think it was a pleasant divorce. My dad got to dance and my mum kept her little boy.

The guitar for me was always a tool for expression. I never really had any of those teenage angst situations, because I always had this escape valve. I found out about teenage angst later on. Some of my friends would smash people over the head with bottles or commit random acts of violence. A lot of this emanates from frustrating situations of oncoming adulthood. There's hormones and the opposite-sex thing happening because of puberty, and all of a sudden you have a little more knowledge and experience. There's a lot of self-discovery happening at this time, and therein lies teenage angst. I never really experienced those frustrations about not knowing how to express myself. I think it's because I was expressing myself through artistic means. That's the only thing I can put it down to, because I wasn't as pissed off about life as some of my friends were. Case in point: a guy I had known since I was about four years old committed suicide when he was about twenty after coming back from a tour of duty in the army. He was always a tortured soul and overly intelligent. But he had a real dark side. I remember when the school hamster died. He suggested that we all go over to his house and cremate it. That's pretty deep thinking for a seven year old, but he did it just to fuck with the girls that were present, who started crying. Mission accomplished. But when you think about it, what the fuck are a bunch of seven year olds doing on their own in a house anyway? I'd had some other friends who committed suicide, not necessarily a teenage angst thing, but probably more due to a general dissatisfaction with life.

Since I was a young kid I always fantasized about visiting America. After all those years of soaking up so much American pop culture, from the music, to movies, to Levi's jeans, to TV shows I loved, like *Rawhide* and *Batman*, I was dying to go to the States. We had such huge access on our black-and-white TVs to all things American. It wasn't uncommon to hear American accents and view American mannerisms because of what I had seen on TV. This was nowhere more evident than in the music we were listening to. Everything was influenced by American pop music. The Beatles, the Who, the Stones, etc. were paying homage to their American idols. That's how they would sing the songs; hence, that became the way we sang. That pretty much answers the question that I'm always asked by Americans, which is *Why do you guys sing with American accents but you don't speak with one?*

Once I got it in my head that I might be able to actually travel to the States, all I needed was money. Together with Jeff, one of the guys I worked with at Profile Typesetters, and my cousin Dave, we took advantage of an amazing air-line deal on Laker Airways. Sir Freddie Laker was a British airline entrepreneur. He was one of the first to adopt the no-frills business model for airlines. Laker made it possible to do a round trip to the States for sixty-six quid, which was less than a hundred bucks back then. So we did it. In 1975 (or '76 – I can't really say for sure), we flew to New York City. From the moment I set foot in America I was in total awe. None of us had ever seen skyscrapers before or any-thing like Times Square. We went to the Statue of Liberty and climbed up into the crown. It was humid, metallic and sweaty inside. Everything really was larger than life.

Then, just like something out of a Chuck Berry song, we got on a Greyhound bus and started motoring west. We visited Chicago, St Louis, Las Vegas and San Francisco (where we stayed at the notorious YMCA), among other cities. We spent a good couple of weeks visiting as many places as we could, and while no one could see all of the country in that amount of time, I felt like we at least made a dent and got a chance to see first-hand many of the things that I had dreamed about – from the Empire State Building to the Golden Gate Bridge. We slept on the bus most nights. We actually broke down just outside Vegas. It was really fucking hot, but they sent another bus to come and get us. America was fascinating. Each state was as different to the next as countries varied in Europe, and I was having the best time ever. There was not just one kind of American person or personality. I also loved all the different styles of music. There was soul music, the little jazz clubs in the bigger cities, country and bluegrass down south, Chicago Blues, all of the great pop music being made in New York and Los Angeles. But best of all for me was the fact that this was where rock music was born. We were tourists, yet there was something about the trip that made me feel right at home. I had a sense that someday I would be back to spend a lot more time here.

Rock music, derived from the blues, is prevalent everywhere in American society. It is practically in every American's DNA. Yet at that time the British yearned for it; bands like Led Zeppelin, the Beatles and the Stones were faithful disciples of what Americans took for granted. That's why Mick Jagger and Keith Richards would wait at the train station for each other with blues records in hand to share with one another in this exclusive 'club'. And that's how I felt. In England we had to seek it out. We had *The Old Grey Whistle Test* and *Top of the Pops*. Think of those shows as England's equivalent of Dick Clark's *American Bandstand* and Don Cornelius's *Soul Train*. They were our only music TV shows. We had one radio station, BBC Radio One, a family station. That was it. We had to search it out – discover it. And that made music mystical and exciting. America was the home of it all.

That said, once we got home to England, it was back to work delivering proofs for Profile Typesetting, and I was totally cool with that. Like I have always said, the day job was a means to an end. I always viewed my early jobs as temporary. I knew I was going to be doing something else. I was going to play music for a living. The guys at Profile were *really* supportive, above and beyond, of my passion for becoming a working musician. I once fell asleep at the wheel at a traffic light somewhere in London because I had been playing a gig the night before. The guys said, 'Just sleep it off.' This support would continue until my band Girl finally got a record deal. Then I could quit my day job. But before that I would go through a few other bands to get to that stage.

One night I was hanging out with Fred Ball, one of my best friends from school, who was a great singer and drummer. We caught this really cool blues/rock band called Tush, obviously based on the ZZ Top song, in Stoke Newington in East London. Tush were about to break up. Their lead guitarist and singer, George Junor, was relocating back to his home town of Glasgow in Scotland. So Mickey Tickton, Tush's bass player, became the new lead singer in the band. I somehow ended up playing guitar, with Tony Miles on guitar and Bob White on drums. Bob eventually left the band and Fred joined. We did a few gigs around London before we ended up as a three piece – Fred, Mickey Tickton and me. By now I was about nineteen years old. Ironically, I reconnected with Bob White in New Zealand in 2011 and with Tony in 2012. Both are doing well, and we had a blast reminiscing over old times. I speak to Fred regularly, too, and he still makes me laugh till I can't breathe. He's one of my oldest friends.

FRED BALL: OK, here goes. We met in the playground of Sir George Monoux boys' school. It was in our first year there. Two boys named Steve Crossley and Gary Saint found out through the school grapevine that I was a drummer and began pitching my knowledge and taste in music against their friend Phil, who played guitar. I was actually messing around in a little band that had a guitarist called Steve Hewer, who always claimed to have taught Phil how to play. Phil and I collaborated on a few fledgling projects: Cheap Thrills was one; Seagoat was another. Seagoat entered a talent competition at the Green Man pub in Leytonstone, London, and won it playing 'Too Rolling Stoned' by Robin Trower. Then Phil sent an audition cassette to UFO [hoping to replace Michael Schenker] but was unsuccessful. We eventually formed a band with Pete Webb, a bass player who was younger than us, and a guy named Jeff Hepting, who was the son of a school caretaker. It was in the school that we began to rehearse. It was the late seventies, coming out of glam rock, which we loved, and going into punk, which we also loved. We were always poncing about with our hair, highlighting and bleaching it until my girlfriend's dad, Cliff Norris Sr, said, 'You look like a load of dumb blondes,' and the original Dumb Blondes were born. We played the pub circuit and the occasional university. We recorded a demo at De Lane Lea studios in Wembley and were presented to various music-biz folk by our managers, Victor Andretti and Vernon Sollas. Despite some great times and naïve fumblings, we achieved only a mild cult status, and Phil was soon off auditioning with various people until he joined Girl. Obviously Phil is a brilliant musician, the best it has been my privilege to know and play with. (You should see the shower of shite I'm with now – only joking.) He did in the early days have a problem with tuning his guitar. It was a Gibson SG and it was in tune when he bought it! I hope my rambling memories can be of help. I won't bore you with birds, booze, and burger stories, but will only mention, 'God, you're a beautiful creature.'

Doing a complete 180, Tush morphed seamlessly into the Dumb Blondes, which was me and Fred's wet dream of getting a glam-rock band together. We recruited Pete Webb, a bass player who had played with me in Lucy, and Jeff Hepting, a lead singer who had never sung before. Jeff was my buddy, who I'd hang out with. We'd date all the same chicks. His audition was us telling him, 'You be the singer.' The other person we kept from the Tush era was our manager, who was an ex-boxer who had bought a pub called the Spread Eagle in Hoxton. Now it's a trendy area, but it used to be really rough back in the days. He also opened up a restaurant called the Ringside Café. His name was Victor Andretti.

Vic looked like a lightweight version of Robert De Niro in *Raging Bull*. He was a former British lightweight champion. Initially upon meeting Victor you'd think he was a bit intimidating. He had the flat nose and the thick cockney accent. Vic was from London's East End. The Spread Eagle was our base. It was at the beginning of Hackney Road, not far from where Jack the Ripper committed many of his murders. We rehearsed and played there. I think a lot of sports guys end up running bars and pubs because they have the know-how and patience to keep shit in check if things get out of order. It was perfect for him and his buddy Joe Lucy, another former boxer, who also used to run a pub called the Ruskin Arms Hotel in East Ham. Vic would call Joe, and then Joe would book us at the Ruskin Arms to play a gig. This would also be the place where I would meet my good friend Rudi Riviere, who would teach me how to do the Eddie Van Halen finger-tap technique on the guitar.

Stevie Marriott and the Small Faces had their first meeting there before it became famous as a heavy metal performance space for early versions of Status Quo, Iron Maiden and other soon-to-be metal legends. The Dumb Blondes tried to mix punk with glam rock, but I think we ended up looking more like construction workers in drag.

RUDI RIVIERE: As a couple of penniless guitar mates who cut our teeth on a staple diet of mid-seventies glam rock and with the unrelenting belief and financial support of his mum, Connie, I watched a lad driven by a zest to succeed and do what he needed to do in order to achieve his goal. We all had phrases and nicknames. Mine was Rudi 'I Go Where My Rock 'n' Roll Takes Me' Riviere, whilst Phil was plain old simple . . . Phil. On one occasion we passed ourselves off as brothers for half an hour, which was no mean feat, as I'm a black man. Once we heard Leppard had recruited Phil, I witnessed such jealousy and backstabbing, I found myself defending my mate in his absence for years to come. The boy had done good! Looking back, maybe I was the weirdo, because to this day, I have been happy and proud to say Phil Collen is a mate of mine.

The glam thing – dyeing our hair, painting our fingernails and wearing mascara – all started when we were about fourteen years old and completely influenced by the Bowie/T. Rex era. It kept going with the emergence of punk rock. So it seemed really normal for us to dye our hair, wear make-up and play in a rock band. At first our parents were a bit weirded out, but it passed quickly when they saw what we were trying to emulate. We'd borrow our girlfriends' clothes and make-up. This was a regular thing for us, although it did raise a few eyebrows at the Ringside Café.

We wanted to be theatrical and one day found out that KISS used pyrotechnics. So we went to the theatrical store and bought some gunpowder. We tested it out in my back garden and blew a crater in the lawn. We almost blew up Fred's mum's front door. We figured we should use a little bit less when we did our gig at the Ruskin Arms, so we stole a metal trash can from someone's front door and wired all of this stuff up for the moment of our entrance to the stage. However, some silly twat tripped the explosive off before we even went onstage, sending hot metal and shrapnel all over the pub. The place was filling up and had a few bikers and locals in there. Thank God it wasn't full, because it would have been carnage. Pete Webb kept his cool, though. He was always a pretty calm and laid-back guy. After all, he was a bass player.

PETE WEBB: It was about 1975 when Phil placed an advert in *Melody Maker* looking for a bass player for a local rock band. I lived in Walthamstow, London, with my parents, and on answering the ad discovered that Phil lived with his parents on the boundary of Walthamstow and Leyton, about a mile and a half away. How nervous I felt as Phil and another young guy turned up on my doorstep one evening. They had ridden over on Phil's motorbike he had then — a Honda 250, I recall? I was about fifteen. Anyway, I distinctly remember playing along to Slade, Sweet and other glam-pop tunes (rather well, I must add), but then Phil asked me if I knew of any Deep Purple songs! I didn't, but I didn't want him to realize my naïvety, so I said that I knew of them but hadn't had a chance to learn any yet!

Well, they said fine and that they would be in touch, and to be quite honest I thought that I had blown it, but was intrigued to find out more about this so-called Deep Purple band! (I must admit, the only heavy rock band I had heard of was Uriah Heep, because they were local, and to this day they are still one of my favourites.)

A day or two later I got a call from Phil saying he was impressed (either that or they never had any luck in finding anyone else) and would I be interested in joining his new band and could I pop around to his address? Well, of course I said yes, and when I got there I remember being invited into the front lounge, which wasn't a lounge, as it was just full up with musical equipment, records, guitars, cassettes, and a couple of speakers and amps.

There were a couple of other dudes there who I had never seen before (who later became my bandmates). Phil was strumming along to a couple of tunes, and then he put on 'Highway Star' and played the riff exactly how it was on the record, but I was waiting for the solo and thought that he would probably improvise around to that. Fuck me! It was exact! Even the second part of the solo, where it speeds up! I had never heard anyone play like that apart from on record. I knew then that I had to pull my socks up and stay around with this guy. He's for real and he's going to be going places.

I was still stunned and flabbergasted over what I had witnessed when Phil's mum, Connie, came in and offered tea and biscuits. I was just as amazed, as she had been in the other room with Phil's nan, watching television. *Is this for real?* I thought. *How can this guy get away with having all these people round, playing rock albums, and playing guitar, while in the very room next door, some sort of normal home life is going on!* I quickly learnt that Connie was absolutely 200 per cent behind Phil's playing. She was every young boy's dream of an ideal mum to have when you were trying to break into this crazy world, instead of saying, 'Why don't you go and get a real job and stop making all that racket?' Connie became a mother to all of us in the future. She would later take in our stage pants and clothes for us! I think Phil's nan used to moan a lot, though, and many a time Connie would argue with her and stick up for what her son was doing. Pity his nan wasn't around for when Phil hit the big time.

Unlike what most young people may have gone through when faced with telling their parents they want to make music for a living, I had total support from my mum and dad. My mum accompanied me to my school for Career Day. I told the career officer that I wanted to be a guitarist, to which he replied, 'Well, you can't do that. But if you're interested in that, then maybe you can work in a guitar factory or a guitar shop.' When we left the school, my mum said, 'Fuck them.' It was the first time I had ever heard her use a swear word in a sentence directed at me. So fuck them I did.

My dad was our roadie. He'd drive us to gigs in his van. My mum would make breakfast for all the guys when they'd come over and stay at the house after the gigs. Even before I was in Def Leppard, Steve Clark and Joe Elliott would come down and stay on the couch at Connie's – we'd become friends by being on the scene together. They'd get tea and bacon 'sarnies' (sandwiches). I had total support around me. The support translated into belief. Even then I could feel that I didn't have that worry. Even to this day, after everything I've been through, I still remember what that feels like. It's a rare thing.

But even with all the encouragement, the Dumb Blondes' days were numbered. While Victor would score us the odd gig at the Marquee Club or the Music Machine (an amazing circa-1900 theatre infamous for being the spot where AC/DC's Bon Scott drank the night he died), and even managed to get us on the cover of the infamous British tabloid *The Sun*, the Dumb Blondes just really didn't have what it took to break through.

At this time, London was exploding with music and culture. You'd bump into Billy Idol, the Pistols, the Damned and Lemmy Kilmister of Motörhead, or hear Elvis Costello and the Police playing live in a pub on any given night. Music was just oozing out of every bar and club. As such an exciting musical period was happening, I felt that we had kind of run our course. I was driven and ambitious. I didn't feel that we were going to move forward any more. In 1978 I hit my twenty-first birthday and said, 'Fuck! I'm still not doing anything.' I felt old for the first time in my life and like I was missing out.

Shortly thereafter, I answered an ad in *Melody Maker* magazine for a 'peroxide guitarist'. The band was called Girl. Phil Lewis and Gerry Laffy looked different from anyone else I had ever met. They looked like they were famous androgynous rock stars. I found out that they were into exactly the same things I was into. It was hard rock, but they had fused all the elements of glam and punk the right way. Also, I had never met anyone who could manipulate people with their sexuality, which these two did naturally and effortlessly. I fitted straight in. They kind of looked like I did – long blond hair and eyeliner. And they had a plan. I showed up to the audition with my Les Paul and Marshall amp. The rest is history . . .

GERRY LAFFY: Philip Lewis and I had various line-ups before we met Phil. We had listed an ad in *Melody Maker (the* music forum at the time in the UK) for a 'peroxide guitarist'. At the time, we rented a restaurant in Camden Lock to rehearse in. We had spoken to this real East End bloke, Phil, who said he was in a band called Dumb Blondes but was very ambitious. An old bashed-up Cortina pulled up, a smiling handsome bleach-blond lad strode up. "Ello, I'm Phil." Yes he was, indeed. Together we lugged up his Marshall 4x12, head, Les Paul. By the time we'd rolled a spliff, he was set up – BANG! Fuck me. Philip and I looked at each other: 'This *is* the guy.' His playing was a cross of Ritchie Blackmore and Al Di Meola. This was 1979! I hadn't yet heard of this new bloke Van Halen. He wanted in, for sure a done deal. Girl proper was born. He brought a song, 'Spiders Web', nice, but not quite us. He had 'Hollywood Tease' in there somewhere and soooo much more yet to come. I have never met a straight man so comfortable in pumps! Later, after the 'My Number', 'You Really Got Me', 'Doctor Doctor', 'You Take Me Dancing' demos were done, we did a video at a porn studio in Muswell Hill. Two cameras, cheap. We thought, *Labels need to see us as well as hear us*. Phil strode in wearing a Chinese blouse and red suede stilettos. *Good on him*, we thought. He just *so* wanted to be a guitar hero, a bit o' slip 'n' camp didn't bother him at *all*. As with all bands, we bonded as family.

We would hang. Basically we'd go out to network and make connections. The band would end up in clubs like Legends, Monkberry's and the Embassy meeting all sorts of people – movie directors, models, actors, the whole nine yards in a completely different circle that I had no idea existed. Gerry and Phil would work it like pros. All of this was for the greater good of the band.

We wanted to get attention because we looked different. We decided to do a cheap performance video so we wouldn't have to slog around the live venue circuit doing gigs. We were creatively skipping a step up the ladder. The studio we managed to blag was actually a gay porn studio in Muswell Hill, complete with bondage and torture accoutrements. It only cost a hundred quid, so it worked out perfect. We filmed about five songs that were to become our résumé. Phil Lewis's then girlfriend was Britt Ekland, a Bond girl and Swedish screen legend. Phil convinced Britt we were the best thing since sliced bread, and she secured us a record deal. We hadn't even done a gig yet. Between her connections and our non-pornographic porn videos, we got a deal with Jet Records, which was owned by Sharon Osbourne's father, Don Arden.

Around this time, a new subculture was emerging in England. Influenced by the punk explosion but having nothing to do with it, the new wave of British heavy metal started producing bands such as Iron Maiden, Saxon, etc. They were hard-rock metal bands but without the overindulgence and twenty-minute-long songs that classic rock bands were producing at the time. These were like four-minute songs played with a renewed fervour. The audience was mainly pubescent boys in leather jackets. The New

Wave of British Heavy Metal (or NWOBHM, as it would come to be known) movement was basically pimply-faced seventeen-year-old boys discovering a music that they could call their own. Unlike their older brothers, who were into hard rock like Zeppelin and Purple, all of a sudden there was a style of music that they could call their own. This was similar to when my generation discovered Bowie and T. Rex. Girl was a hybrid of hard rock and extreme glam. This didn't go over well with sexually frustrated pubescent boys in leather jackets. So when Girl came mincing about onstage and in the press, it really upset a lot of these rock fans. We never felt like we had anything to do with the movement. We just happened to come out at the same time as Def Leppard, who unfortunately got lumped in with NWOBHM, even though they had nothing to do with it. It was just the time and the place.

Contrary to popular mythology, I didn't really hang out in that whole beer-drinking, leather-jacket-wearing NWOBHM environment unless we happened to be playing in one of those venues. My scene was quite different from where people may have thought I was hanging. We were hanging out in gay nightclubs – not because we were gay per se, but because it was the complete opposite of a male-dominated homophobic rock movement and a lot more fun.

It wasn't long before our audiences, especially in the London area, morphed into that pseudo club scene of really hot model-type girls. Unlike the Dumb Blondes, Girl didn't look like truckers with make-up on. The more feminine we looked, the more females turned up at our shows. Tons of girls, including hordes of Japanese females who actually travelled from Japan after seeing us in their magazines, would show up at our London Marquee shows. We were there quite often and in fact did a residency twice. There was also a band called Japan that was out at the same time. We all loved that band, but the rock audiences hated them because theirs was an eclectic blend of various styles of music. We kind of modelled our look on Japan-meets-New York Dolls. But we were actually a hard-rock band. So for some reason it definitely gave us credibility with girls, not to mention we came over as being pretty sexy.

Our very first showcase rehearsal was at a soundstage in Shepperton film studios with a full lighting rig and sound system. We performed for all of the record company executives and they loved it.

Now it was time to do our first gig. We played our first live show at the Music Machine, located in Camden Town. A lot of the British rock press turned out because our record company had already generated a lot of hype about us, which coincided with the release of our first single, 'My Number'. We got slagged off for that because apparently people felt we hadn't paid our dues. Then, after recording about half of *Sheer Greed*, we left for my very first tour, opening for UFO in Europe.

My first tour was an education in everything. It was like being thrown in the deep end. I had never done the city-to-city thing, seeing all of these new places like France, Germany, the Netherlands, Belgium, etc. We were driving in a station wagon with Liam, our tour manager, through the snow and rain. UFO really took us under their wing. We got fucked-up every single night. There were all of these European women I had never seen before. By this time, Simon Laffy, Gerry's older brother, had become the bassist in Girl. Simon actually played bass on our first album, *Sheer Greed*. Simon's bass style was more elaborate. He could play funk, jazz and finger-style bass. His musical tastes were varied, like mine. He could listen to George Duke one minute, then the Police the next. He definitely added another dimension to the band. We were a lot more musical. I'd met Simon before he was in the band. Since he was Gerry's brother and flatmate, we'd already been hanging out.

SIMON LAFFY: I first met Phil during the summer of 1979, at a Girl rehearsal in Camden Lock. I wasn't in the band at that time but was always closely linked to its development because it was started by my brother, Gerry. I was particularly blown away by Phil's ferocious soloing – I felt it sounded like an intoxicating blend of Jimi Hendrix, Ritchie Blackmore and Al Di Meola (*Return to Forever* period). He seemed to effortlessly combine shameless attention-seeking with virtuoso lead playing and, to me, was clearly a natural-born rock star.

One of my fondest memories of this period was of visiting Phil's adorable mother, Connie. After gigs or rehearsals, we would all pile back to her house in East London to eat a takeaway curry ('Ruby Murray', in cockney rhyming slang) and watch the latest horror movie on pirate video (then known as 'video nasties'). Fortunately, the actual quality of these videos was so nasty that poor Connie was spared the worst of the blood and gore – you literally could not see through all the distortion and blur! It seems quite laughable now, in the context of present-day illegal downloading and the plethora of pirate websites, but at that time, we thought we were such rebels watching pirate movies.

Phil Lewis and I were twenty-two years old. Simon Laffy, Gerry's brother, was twenty; Gerry was nineteen; and Dave Gaynor, our drummer, was also twenty-two. It was pretty hardcore driving around Europe getting to the next gig. I had never really stayed in a hotel before. We were throwing up, drunk off our asses, and still performing all over Europe. It was a brand-new experience that I was living that I had only heard about. I can remember being in Germany at a hotel when Phil Mogg, UFO's lead singer, and someone else broke into a kitchen, stole a shark's head out of the fridge and tried to put it into someone's bed à la *The*

*Godfather*. We got caught because a food fight ensued in the kitchen. It's all a little bit blurry, but I'm sure it happened. Even though there were tons of laughable moments, UFO gave us lots of great advice about performing, like pacing ourselves, set lists, and all the little nuances that can make a show better for the audience. The UK leg of this tour is also where I met the photographer Ross Halfin, whose photos you can see in this very book. Ross and I are friends to this day.

Around this time, I met my first serious girlfriend Liz at the London nightclub Monkberry's. Monkberry's was a bizarre mix of models, actors and Arab princes, and had a heavily gay overtone. It was very hip and very chic, and was the first venue where Grace Jones played in London.

Liz was holding court and was the hottest girl I had ever seen in the flesh up to that point. I couldn't quite figure out what her ethnicity was. I thought she was a mixed black girl. She had really full lips, brown skin and a mass of curly black hair. I was trying to figure out how to approach this person who was talking to all these people. I finally got her number and found out that she was a West End Jewish girl, as she says to people when they start speaking to her in Spanish. We started going out. Liz became very important in my life early on because she would always have my back and I would have hers. No matter how well things seemed to be progressing, I was still a broke-ass musician. Liz would always make sure I had enough money to put gas in my car.

She would work and put money toward me getting my career going. Even though we had this on-again, off-again relationship through the years, she would always be there if I needed her. In fact, it was Liz who took care of my mum and held her hand as she died while I was on a plane on my way in from the States to London. She was also instrumental in getting my dad to the hospital when he was diagnosed with terminal cancer. Liz raised hell for my dad in that hospital, and to this day she is one of my dearest friends. (She even managed to come up with the design that became the cover of the Def Leppard *X* album sleeve.) She's now happily married to a wonderful guy named Gary who works as a psychotherapist in London. I'm so glad that she has finally found Gary. All it took was his letting Liz be amazing Liz, something I couldn't quite seem to do.

Girl's debut single, 'My Number', premiered on the John Peel show on BBC's Radio One. Our second single, 'Hollywood Tease', made it into the UK charts. When *Sheer Greed* came out in January 1980, we found ourselves on my favourite TV show, *The Old Grey Whistle Test*. We also performed on *Top of the Pops*. How strange it was to be standing on that stage, playing that show that I'd watched so many times as a kid. It was hard to fathom that our band really seemed to be taking off.

In 1980 we did a club tour of England. This was after we did the European tour with UFO. We had TV appearances and an album in the charts, so now it was time to strike out on tour on our own. This would have been from the Marquee in London to the Mayfair in Newcastle and everywhere in between. It seemed a little strange showing up to gigs in Britt Ekland's white Rolls-Royce. I can clearly remember me, Phil, Britt and Doris Tyler, who looked after Britt, rolling up to a tiny club in this car. We didn't do the whole tour in the Rolls, but it was absolutely a blast and completely out of context. But that was really what this band was. We were contrary to what everyone else did. Because of the circles we were moving in, it would always attract really cool people and really sleazy people.

In the summer of 1980, we played the Reading Festival, before 35,000 people. Obviously the biggest crowd I'd ever played in front of. Bryson Graham was on drums. Bryson had played with George Harrison, Peter Frampton and Spooky Tooth when he was very young. So here we were with our biggest crowd ever. These British rock festival audiences at the time were notorious for throwing giant beer cans filled with piss and all sorts of stuff onto the stage. The first thing that came onstage, I remember Bryson wanting to dive into the audience to start fighting. Gerry screamed for him to sit down and carry on. We realized that if we completely ignored the audience, they would stop throwing stuff and we'd have a cool show, and we did. This is something I definitely keep in mind to this day while performing. Def Leppard got it the next night.

\*

The first time I ever tried coke was sometime during 1979 or 1980. I was petrified because I'd never done anything before that besides drinking. But after that it seemed pretty easy, and plus this shit was flowing everywhere. There was heroin, acid, Mandies . . . I tried it all. The first time I snorted heroin, I threw up all over the floor. I was at someone's house (can't recall whose). But it wasn't the last time. I'd get carried away doing this stuff. I can remember doing heroin on the beach in Blackpool and then throwing up onstage. I never missed a beat. I totally understood the buzz with heroin, because it made you feel great – numbed you out. But the projectile vomiting wasn't much fun. An incident like that at Blackpool, although extreme, was rare. I did a massive line of what I thought was cocaine once, but it turned out to be Chinese white heroin. Once I did some acid in the afternoon whilst recording and it didn't kick in till the show that night in Gravesend. I got through it, but I don't remember too much except I laughed a lot. I definitely mellowed out onstage after this tour. It's not cool going out and playing like that and not remembering anything.

I wasn't really a druggie or an alcoholic, although I enjoyed the getting fucked-up part with anyone who was around me. Over the years, I found out the difference between addicts, alcoholics and the occasional user. I feel fortunate that I got out fairly unscathed. Unfortunately for a lot of people, once they start going down this road, they can't stop or turn off. As for me back then, of course there were lots of drug and alcohol 'binges', most of which I can't even remember, so don't expect a lot of details about them, because in those days it wasn't like I was getting fucked-up to remember anything years later.

Through all the insanity, we played on. And we gradually noticed a shift in our audience, as we became known around town. Our best gigs, I think, were when we did residencies at the London Marquee. There would be all these luminaries – actors and models – showing up. We'd think, *Oh, this is really cool. Everyone really likes us.* Then we realized they were coming for the booty. I may not have got into rock and roll for women, but in Girl there was really no choice. Women were everywhere. Phil Lewis's on- and off-stage magnetism created this dynamic whereby we would have dozens of gorgeous girls waiting for us after every show. There'd be guys from Thin Lizzy and Queen. Ritchie Blackmore's band came one night and he was ogling Liz, so we invited him onstage. I got to jam with my guitar hero. We played 'Born to Be Wild', and he played my black Fender Strat, a twenty-first-birthday present from my mum. Eventually, it was to be the main guitar on *Hysteria*.

It was around this time that we started working on our second album. We hooked up with Peter Maddock and Danny Secunda as our managers. Instead, we probably should have taken Don Arden & Co. up on their management offer. Their plan for the band seemed to have more drive. The Maddock/Secunda plan took us further away from what we did on the first album. The second record wasn't that good. When we were with the major label (Jet was affiliated with CBS in the States), everything was classier. Girl needed structure. I really do believe that Girl, with more nurturing, could have done something really special, just like Def Leppard, nurtured as we were by Mutt Lange, Peter Mensch and Cliff Burnstein. We didn't have that with Girl, and everything started slipping away.

# 2

The first time I heard Def Leppard was when I was in Girl and they were played on the radio. It sounded a lot different to all the other bands that were out at the time, because there were really rich harmonies to go along with the catchy songs. The first time I met Def Leppard was when they came to the Music Machine in Camden Town to see our first Girl gig. I think the whole band was there – Joe Elliott, Steve Clark, Rick Allen, Rick 'Sav' Savage and Pete Willis – and they came backstage to say hi. The fact that we were all coming out in the music papers at the same time meant we all knew who the other was. It was competitive, but as far as the guys in Def Leppard went, they seemed genuinely nice, and although they had funny accents – well, Sheffield is a long way from Hackney – I was pulling for their success. Interestingly enough, when I first joined the band, I would find myself lip-reading Rick

Allen because his accent was so strong. It's funny what thirty years will do to each other's accents, as we all have blended into one while somehow managing to keep a version of our original accents intact.

When they headlined the Lyceum, we made sure to send them a congratulatory telegram. Remember those? And we ended up having some really interesting experiences together. There was the time after Girl opened for Pat Travers at Sheffield City Hall when Joe and Steve Clark joined me and Phil Lewis at a local club and went up onstage to play a bunch of classic rock covers. Then we all ended up sleeping in Joe's mum and dad's spare room, inspiring that now famous quote from Joe's mum, Cindy Elliott, 'Ohhhh! There was make-up in the bed this morning when I changed the sheets!' Another night in London at the Music Machine, Joe and Steve joined me and Phil again onstage with future Iron Maiden front man Bruce Dickinson, who was then in a band called Samson. We did a killer version of Zeppelin's 'Whole Lotta Love'.

JOE ELLIOTT: Back when Def Leppard was first getting started, the one local band that stood out to me was Girl. OK, so it didn't hurt that their lead singer, Phil Lewis, was with Britt Ekland. But it went much further than that. They reminded me of so much that was not happening at the time. It seemed like every other band was dressing like Iron Maiden, but these guys looked like true rock stars. In fact, they seemed more like Rod Stewart. And while they weren't quite Japan, they were aware of who the band Japan was.

I saw them on TV when they performed on the *Whistle Test*, and they were just amazing. They were snotty and had this great pop rock sound. They just had a sparkling presence. They could play hard and they could also play soft. They were not just straight-ahead hard rock. For me, this gave them a sort of Bowie edge that really intrigued me.

I wanted to go out of my way to hear them live, and so when I saw that they were opening for UFO at the nearby Sheffield City Hall, I knew I just had to go. I didn't go there that night just to meet Phil Collen. I was there to see all five guys. But then backstage after the show, Phil Lewis, Phil Collen and Steve Clark and I decided to go to a little discotheque called Genevieve's. There was a lot of dancing there, but bands also played, and on this particular night there was a group called Sledgehammer. After they finished their set, we asked if we could borrow their gear to play a few songs onstage. Nobody knew who we were, and we were just having a bit of fun. Phil Lewis handled the lead vocals, the other Phil played guitar, Steve played bass, and I sat in behind the drum kit, which I could basically play anyway. I remember that we played the KISS song 'Do You Love Me?' because it was something that Girl had just recorded. And it actually sounded pretty good, even though we were basically pissed out of our minds.

That night, the guys from Girl were booked to stay in a hotel out in the countryside about twenty miles away. But it was two o'clock in the morning, which meant it would have been a real haul to get there. So I let them stay at my mum and dad's house.

We did not have a spare bedroom, so I told them that they would be sharing a bed, and they were drunk enough to just say fine. My dad was up to work early the next morning, so he never saw them, but my mum met them and liked them quite a bit. They played with her little Yorkshire terrier and she found Phil and Phil quite charming.

After they left, she went to make the bed and noticed make-up all over the pillowcase. She thought I had snuck some girls into the house over the night, but I had to explain to her that these guys were a band that wore make-up, kind of like Marc Bolan or the New York Dolls.

Phil Collen and I exchanged numbers that morning, and I had a pretty good idea that he and I would be staying in touch. We seemed to have a pretty similar view on the local music scene and how the press handled everything. He was refreshing. At that time around Sheffield you had the Human League, Thompson Twins, ABC – in Def Leppard, we were like the outside stepchildren.

Sometime in 1981 I got a strange call from Joe Elliott one day while I was at my mum's house in Walthamstow. Def Leppard were out on tour, opening up for Ozzy Osbourne in the States, and things, according to Joe, weren't really working out with Pete Willis. Joe said, 'Can you learn sixteen songs in two days?' Of course I replied, 'Yeah.' I mean, even though I was still in Girl, I was sure all the guys would have been cool with me helping Def Leppard out on their US tour. But Joe called back the next day and said they had smoothed things over.

But back to Girl . . . Then, of course, there were the gigs we played with KISS, their last shows before taking the make-up off that first time. Gene Simmons was dating Diana Ross at the time. He introduced us to her (and impressed us at the same time – by remembering all of our names). I was happy to meet her but I thought, *Wow! The shiny and expensive Diana Ross is here with us in this shithole at Bingley Hall,* a venue in Birmingham. Bingley Hall was quite interesting for a few reasons. We had an all-male audience. Joe Elliott came to see us. We got spat at like we were the Clash, and to top it all off I got rip-roaring drunk, had sex with a girl and threw up all over her while I was fucking her. Bingley Hall.

Toward the end of Girl, we were doing some pretty creative stuff. We were getting studio time in this great little studio called Matrix that was owned by Nigel Frieda, brother of the ultra-famous hair designer John Frieda. Nigel was ultra-cool. He would call us if a band cancelled or finished early so we could get the graveyard shift for free or a limited price. We'd show up at one in the morning or 6 a.m., whenever we got the call. We did some really cool demos there. It was around this time I got a phone call from Paul Di'Anno, Iron Maiden's lead singer, who I had known since I was six from when we went to school together. He asked if I'd be interested in joining the band, as Dennis Stratton, one of Maiden's guitarists, had just left. I mentioned it to the guys in Girl. Not for selfish reasons, but they really didn't think it would be the right choice for me. But before I got a chance to respond to Paul, Adrian Smith joined the band. That's ironic, actually, because Adrian is one of the five people who we considered for a guitarist after Steve passed. He's a great guy who successfully merged back into Iron Maiden.

My last gig with Girl was a show at the Zig Zag club in London in 1982 with drummer Pete Barnacle, who was the best fit for the band. The Zig Zag was an interesting space. *Zig Zag* was a London magazine that decided to open a live music venue under the same name. It was located at 22–24 Great Western Road, London, and was open for just a year. All of the guys from Def Leppard had come down to watch the show. I decided to just go crazy with my guitar that night and play the wildest solos I could. I played with my teeth and one hand. I played the guitar behind my head and I put on as great a show as I knew how. I put all the Jimi Hendrix tricks out there purely because I was hamming it up for everyone in attendance. Little did I know it was kind of my audition for Def Leppard. It was one of the only times in my life I played semi-drunk, so I was extra-uninhibited up there and had an amazing show. The irony of that was that Def Leppard were replacing someone in their band who had problems with alcohol.

In June of 1982 Joe phoned me up and asked if I would like to come down and play a couple of solos on the new Def Leppard album. I was already familiar with what they were doing because I had lent the guys an amplifier when they were recording in a studio in Hastings. I said, 'Sure. Absolutely,' not really thinking anything of it. When I showed up, everyone explained what was going on and that it wasn't working out with Pete Willis. By this time, he was drinking excessively, and it had started affecting his playing and the rest of the band. Nothing was really said, because they obviously wanted to see how I would do. The producer Mutt Lange was there. I had met him earlier in the year during the recording of the *High 'n' Dry* album in Hastings and gave me a cassette and said, 'Have a listen to this song and come up with a solo for it.' The song was 'Stagefright'. So I went in the next day, plugged in my fifty-watt Marshall head and just let it rip. It blew everyone away because I got it in the first take, and that's what you hear on the record. From that point on I was asked to do more solos on the tracks that Pete would have played on, i.e. 'Photograph', 'Rock! Rock! (Till You Drop)', 'Foolin', 'Rock of Ages' and then fun lead guitar stuff on 'Billy's Got a Gun' and 'Too Late'. It was a lead guitarist's dream. All the hard work had already been laid down by Steve and Pete. When Mutt found out I could sing, he had me foghorn on everything – stuff like the two-part harmonies that I do with Joe all the time, which can particularly be heard on 'Too Late' and 'Foolin'. Now it's part of our signature sound.

Several days later, with Joe joining me in my old MK3 Ford Cortina, we headed off to Def Leppard manager Peter Mensch's house for a meeting with the band, Peter and Mutt. Peter lived just off Kensington High Street near Holland Park, and by the time we got to his house the stick shift had come off in my hand and we practically drove through his front window.

JOE ELLIOTT: Over the next year or so whenever I would go on to London, I would ring Phil up and we would go to the pub to talk. Or we would crash at each other's homes or apartments. As Def Leppard began to get more popular, Phil and I remained in touch. He was a great guy and we always had interesting conversations.

We knew we were making something really special in the studio, and so when our producer, Mutt Lange, started getting concerned about Pete, we knew something had to give pretty soon. In essence, Mutt was a part of our band, and his voice carried a lot of weight. When we realized that Mutt might actually walk off from working with us because of Pete, we knew we had to do something. And I knew that Phil was the right guy for our band.

So there was one day in 1982 when we sat Pete down and explained to him that it was time to go. It was a bit of a difficult conversation, but I think he was relieved as well, because all of a sudden a lot of pressure was lifted off of him. That same day, we had Phil come down to visit at our manager's house. He pulls up in that old rust bucket of a Ford Cortina and we all have a decent meeting. We play him some of the music we're working on and he gets really excited. He couldn't believe the sounds we were getting in the studio. As we were taught by Mutt, the studio was essentially another band member, and Phil loved that concept.

I should add, what really sealed the deal for me was a performance I'd seen a few weeks before, when Girl played at a place called the Zig Zag club. Phil played about as brilliantly as I had ever seen someone play up close like that. And when I met him backstage afterward, I realized he was completely pissed out of his mind. It struck me: if a guy can play that well being as blitzed as he was, then that really said something.

So before he left our manager's house, Mutt gave Phil a cassette copy of a song we were working on called

'Stagefright'. Phil's assignment was to go home and create a solo for that record, which only had rhythm tracks on it. The next day he came down to the studio where we were working. The rest of us were watching World Cup soccer on TV while Mutt went into the studio to work with Phil. About thirty minutes later Mutt came rushing out excitedly and had us come in to the studio to listen to the solo that Phil had created. It was amazing. It was just the kind of sound and attitude that our band needed to get to the next level.

Once Mutt blessed him, that was it. But I think I always knew in the back of my head that Phil was the right guy.

The meeting was pretty comfortable from the start because I had become friends with the band. Mensch's house was the hang. He was the New Yorker living in London. We'd go around there to drink coffee and talk shit. I had met Mutt years before, and I knew Peter because a year earlier, when I needed some business advice, Joe suggested I speak to him. Mensch was really cool like that. Although he was very busy, he made time to give me some career and business advice related to the whole Girl situation. At this point they were not giving me a formal offer to join the band, at least not that I heard. They just needed some help with the guitars on the album. But then it quickly morphed into, 'Right. So we're going to do a European tour to promote this album. It's going to be called *Pyromania*. You guys had better start rehearsing.' So I packed my stuff up and went to Sheffield. It sounded like a lot of fun. You have to remember at this point Def Leppard were still playing clubs. They were an opening act, and not much bigger than Girl was in England. None of us ever envisioned this as a turning point in our life of what we'd become.

When I went back home and told my girlfriend Liz, she was ecstatic. I was leaning toward accepting the tour offer because of the comfort level that was established so quickly with these guys. Plus, it was a chance to see the world. But any small doubt I had was erased by Liz's enthusiasm. 'I'll never speak to you again if you don't accept this offer,' she told me. 'This is a band that is very disciplined and poised to do great things, and you can help them get there. Everything else you've been doing up until this point has been designed for this moment. You need them and they need you. It's perfect.'

I could not argue with Liz. She was exactly right. The guys in Def Leppard in many ways were like me and vice versa. They approached their music like it was art. They hadn't got into rock and roll for all the cheap thrills. That doesn't mean we didn't enjoy some of the cheap thrills, but their overarching goal was to create music that would last.

There wasn't a solid invitation for me to join the band. About ten years later (I think), Joe finally gave me an official invite into the band, which I promptly declined and still haven't accepted to this day.

LIZ SHORTS: I remember distinctly when he came home and told me about the opportunity to tour with Def Leppard. He was really struggling with the decision and wanted my advice. I like to think he needed my advice. He really loved being in Girl and he was fiercely loyal to his bandmates. I think he had a real hesitation about jumping from the frying pan into the fat. Part of it was, I think he was scared of the unknown. But he was also scared of leaving those guys on their own. They had done so much together, and I know he didn't want to feel like he was abandoning them.

My whole speech to Phil was about helping him understand that there was a vocation at stake. If he wanted to survive as a musician, he had to look at things in terms of what was the best job going to be. I really felt that with Def Leppard he had a bigger chance of going someplace. And I tried to let him know that he wasn't being disloyal if he moved on. Oh sure, I knew the guys would be very pissy at first and that they would certainly be devastated. But they loved Phil just as he loved them. The one thing with all the guys and Girl was that they were very smart. Emotion aside, they knew it was the right thing to do and that they would certainly have done the same thing if they were in Phil's shoes.

Nevertheless, it was not an easy discussion, and Phil and I argued about it for about two weeks. I couldn't stress to him enough to take the touring assignment with

Def Leppard. He would agree with me to a point but then fall back on the loyalty. Finally, I think he understood. He really just needed somebody he trusted to help him get there. And just like I thought, when he told the guys, it was really difficult. But as they began to process the information, they all came around pretty quickly and supported what he was doing. Those things are never easy. When guys are in bands like that, there's a brotherhood that exists that is very sensitive. Part of it was, I think they knew that Phil now had a shot of going on to bigger and better things. They were happy for him. And for Phil it was like he was bidding farewell to some of his favourite friends in the world. But sometimes you just have to look beyond the moment at the bigger picture. To me, Def Leppard was the bigger picture.

I had a discussion with the guys in Girl. They all were in agreement that I should do the Def Leppard tour since it seemed like Girl had plateaued and everything was changing so fast around us.

Back then Def Leppard had hired Mutt, who was one of the greatest, if not the greatest producer in the world at that point, to help them achieve a unique sound, and they were giving me a chance to join the team. I take that word, *team*, very seriously. I noticed right up front that there was a Def Leppard democracy in terms of how responsibilities and achievements were shared equally. This was not a band that was about egos but a band that had a working-class focus on making the best records and creating the best live performances possible. They were ultra-competitive and had an emphasis on musical substance. I was the exact same way.

I also met Malvin Mortimer the first week I started playing with the band. Malvin wasn't just a guitar tech. He took on many other duties, including keeping everyone fed, which was no easy feat considering the various dietary specifications from the band. Bacon, eggs, beans, mushrooms, tomatoes – kind of the typical English fry-up. And nobody was better than Malvin at cooking that up for the guys, but I became a vegetarian at the end of the *Pyromania* tour, and Rick Allen followed suit during the recovery from his accident. So Malvin would simplify things for us. He catered to us and always made us the best English comfort food, like Heinz beans on toast. I quickly learned he was really an extension of the band.

Steve Clark and I liked each other, but we played guitar very differently. We had drastic styles. Listening to *Pyromania*, it was obvious that a guitar orchestra was on hand. To be quite honest, you'd need at least four guitar players to get most of this stuff done. So it was important that we work together. Rehearsals were the beginning of our deep friendship and concepts for a new style of guitar playing. Steve's favourite guitar player was Jimmy Page. I always felt that the genius of Jimmy Page wasn't his lead playing per se but total depth in arrangements and production. People often get confused about Jimmy Page's role. Steve didn't, so he would come up with these wonderful guitar lines that I hadn't heard before. They weren't standard but totally unique. If you add Mutt Lange, plus my guitars, into the mix, we had a whole new style based on a team effort, which most other rock bands didn't seem to do. I didn't really delve into the psyche of the music then because I simply looked at it as a lot of fun. I was twenty-four and thought I was a part of something that, if it didn't do well, would still be OK. It was still something to be proud of. The fulfilment of doing all that overrode the sex, drugs, and rock and roll part of it. During *Hysteria*, that became even more apparent.

I pull a lot of people up on this next point when they say they prefer *High 'n' Dry* to *Pyromania*. I tell them you can still detect other bands in *High 'n' Dry*, as AC/DC had a strong influence on that album, since Mutt had just produced AC/DC. I really do consider Mutt to be a musical genius. I think Def Leppard was a really good band. But Mutt took a really good band and made them great. From the beginning, he had a very clear concept of what he thought we should sound like. And of course as it turned out he was right. His idea for the band was that we would be a cross between AC/DC and Queen but more raw. Mutt told us, 'Def Leppard will be all about great pop songs that resonate with the punk ethos. We won't have lovely harmonies like Styx or Foreigner. Our vocals will be more like a screaming chant, which will set them apart.'

I truly believe Def Leppard was still searching for its identity. *Pyromania* was a departure and way more original sounding because the team had been working constantly. All of a sudden it sounded like Def Leppard. It's amazing that in this day and age bands or artists don't have the luxury of being nurtured and allowed to reach their full potential. We did. The music business became more of a business and less about art. I feel really fortunate to have been around at a time when we could exercise that right. I think *Hysteria* was even more original sounding, and came to epitomize the typical Def Leppard sound, because we had time to take it to a whole other level and we were nurtured to do so. And to be honest, we also had a record label at the time that was prepared to shell out millions of dollars toward recording. *Pyromania* was a stepping-stone. It didn't sound like anyone else. However, the band's true originality, in my opinion, culminated in the *Hysteria* album.

In the States, meanwhile, a fresh and bold forum was taking over the airwaves that would help us maximize our sound and image: MTV. In its early days, MTV played a handful of videos that were rotated to death. In 1982, Joan Jett's 'I Love Rock 'n Roll', the Go-Go's 'We Got the Beat' and

Billy Idol's 'White Wedding' were a few of the most played videos. But MTV was new; there still wasn't that much product out there to fill a twenty-four-hour schedule, and so they had to use what they had. They were hungry for more videos to play, and bands were falling over themselves to make them. It's true, video killed the radio star, and it was exploding on American cable TV. We wanted in.

So before the tour, we filmed videos for what were to be our first two singles off the album – 'Photograph', filmed on 2 December, which was Sav's birthday, and 'Rock of Ages', filmed on 8 December, my twenty-fifth birthday. Both were done at the infamous decommissioned coal-fired plant Battersea Power Station in London. This is the same building on Pink Floyd's *Animals* album cover. Pink Floyd actually rigged an immense inflatable pig between two of the power station's southern chimneys that day, but unfortunately the pig broke loose from its moorings and rose into the flight path of nearby Heathrow airport. Eventually the beast landed harmlessly in Kent, but the band was smart enough to shoot the footage, and it was used in a promo video for the song 'Pigs on the Wing'. Alfred Hitchcock was here in 1936 to shoot the opening scene of his classic film *Sabotage*, and the Beatles even shot here during their 1965 film *Help*.

The power station is a foreboding-looking place, with four industrial smokestacks towering ominously on the south bank of the River Thames, in Battersea, an inner-city district of South-West London. It was built back in the 1930s, and it's been the site of many a production for obvious reasons. It just looks fucking cool.

MTV was just about a year and a half old when we started planning the videos for the two lead singles off *Pyromania*. Our management knew that it would be a good idea for us to have a couple of visual pieces ready when the record was released. Visually, Def Leppard was an interesting band compared to what else was going on back then. We looked different from all the other rock bands out there. People would soon start comparing us to Duran Duran. But the difference was that while Duran Duran had many girls flocking to them, Def Leppard soon had a reputation for getting all the girls *and* their boyfriends. Twice the audience. Instead of shying away from being filmed, as most rock bands did, we embraced it, thus making ourselves MTV video darlings. That was a huge difference. Plus we were a hard-rock band.

As I said above, video did kill the radio star. But having said that, the internet killed the video star. Now we can watch or create anything we want ourselves and share it almost immediately. But back then, we were absolutely at the right place in the right time, as this thing was exploding on American cable TV, with the most infectious blend of hard rock and pop in our lead-off single, 'Photograph'.

Our videos at Battersea were directed by David Mallet, who had a fantastic reputation at the time. He had directed some of the most interesting and groundbreaking videos of all time – a slew of them for Bowie, as well as videos for Boomtown Rats, Blondie and many others. When we arrived at Battersea to film for 'Photograph', we were very impressed with the set that Mallet had created for us. It was very dramatic, with mesh flooring and lights shooting up through the floor and all of these primal cages with girls in torn stockings and ripped tops. Might seem pretty cheesy today, but back then it was one of the coolest things we'd been involved with.

For 'Photograph', we hired a Marilyn Monroe lookalike to create a bit of the storyline, as if the song was about her. Interestingly, there are two versions of this video. A censored version includes a brief knife scene at the beginning; in the alternate version, the knife scene is replaced with the stationary black cat. The whole 'passion killer' lyrical bit allowed Mallet to create a little scenario as if there'd been a murder committed. Just a little bit of plot to keep things interesting. We got banned from British TV, which was amazing, because you could shoot people on camera but God forbid there was a switchblade. The song was cranked out over and over through giant speakers, and we simply lip-synched along, striking poses throughout.

The song 'Rock of Ages' begins with a cartoonish voice that says something like 'Gunter glieben glausen gloeben', and as soon as we heard that the camera started to roll. Just to clarify some age-old trivia here – that's Mutt Lange doing a mock German/Swedish accent instead of saying 'One, Two, Three, Four.' The words mean absolutely nothing. For all you devil worshippers out there, I'm sure I just destroyed a theory.

As far as our fashion instincts in the videos go, it was really just grab bag. In one video shot Joe has on one of his mum's scarves. We all borrowed whatever we could. One interesting detail in both of those videos we were to shoot were the clothes emblazoned with the Union Jack that Joe and Rick wore.

I wore a blue silk shirt and these really tight white pants for the 'Rock of Ages' shoot. I had a full camera shot of me shaking my ass at about twenty-eight seconds into the video. This obviously made an impression, because I was parodied in the cult classic film *This Is Spinal Tap* on the song 'Big Bottom'. Immortalized.

A few weeks before the video shoots, when we were rehearsing for the upcoming tour, Joe and Rick had stopped on Kensington High Street, where Joe picked up a Union Jack T-shirt and Rick got some shorts. This was just at one of those touristy stalls where they sell those things. The Union Jack had become semi-emblematic for bands such as the Who and the Sex Pistols.

But, in recent years, it had become fairly quiet as an iconic rock-and-roll emblem. Well, that was about to change and we hadn't even planned it out. These videos were my first interactions with Def Leppard in any kind of performance. Even though we weren't really playing, it did give us a chance to start getting our performance chops together and figure out where we stood and how we would be in front of people. And when I look back at those videos today, I see us pioneering something. As dated as the videos may look now, something new and exciting was definitely being created.

Once kids saw that emblem in the videos it caught on and eventually we started producing hundreds of thousands of Union Jack items to satisfy the merchandise demand. It was a total fluke. We were like the latest wave of the British Invasion, Part 2. The result of Joe and Rick's decision to shop novelty is still associated with us to this day.

I give Mutt credit even when it came to our videos. This is a guy who really brought rock to the masses. He understood what it took to have this form of music cross over to a much broader audience. That's a real magic of his. Later on he would do it with country music. But he certainly did it with Def Leppard. And when he started making us sound different to Motörhead, Iron Maiden and Judas Priest, it made us feel like we also wanted to look different to them. Those were our contemporaries back then, and they really all looked kind of the same. It was all very black leather and very macho and with spiky bracelets, studs and the like. So here we've got this sort of hybrid album that has the potential to cross over into the pop world, and so we consciously decided to look different, too. We didn't look all tough and macho. We just looked more in line with Duran Duran than Iron Maiden and it really made a difference, making our image a lot more desirable and palatable. It may not seem like that big a deal today, but those videos separated us from the rest of the pack coming out of England.

On 20 January 1983, *Pyromania* was officially released. The initial critical response suggested that we had something special on our hands. This was, in part, how *Rolling Stone* writer David Fricke reviewed the album:

*Just when it seemed like synthesizers had taken over the airwaves, along comes Def Leppard with* Pyromania, *a heavy-metal album full of brawling guitars and boasting state-of-the-radio production. Steve Clark and new member Phil Collen's fat fuzz riffs and power chords are more emotionally charged than most of the synthesized disco that passes for 'modern music,' and Robert John 'Mutt' Lange's work behind the board brings singer Joe Elliott's screaming vocals into focus. But this young band (the average age is twenty-one) demonstrates surprising sophistication [and] manipulates old heavy-metal tricks into tight, invigorating songs while holding epic pretensions in check. Both 'Comin' Under Fire' and 'Photograph' combine the kaboom of AC/DC with slick choruses and brassy vocal harmonies that sound like a gassed-up Boston.*

Not bad at all. All of the cards seemed to be in place. The album was on its way, the videos were shot and in the can, and now all we had to do was get on the road.

The plan was to spend all of February through mid-March touring Europe. We would be playing throughout England, France, Switzerland, Belgium, Ireland and Scotland. Then, in mid-March, we would head to the States for an opening slot on the Billy Squier tour. The year before, Squier had put out the monster album *Emotions in Motion*, on the title track of which he shared vocals with Queen's Freddie Mercury and Roger Taylor. But it was the single 'Everybody Wants You' that had really given Squier arena rock status, and so we were happy with the invitation to play the shows.

MALVIN MORTIMER [tour manager]: A few months earlier Pete Willis had been let go because of his persistent drinking and Phil Collen had been chosen as his replacement, Joe had been a fan of the band Girl (I am sure that Rick Savage had agreed with Joe, so Phil was *in*). In the following months I saw pictures of Phil, in full girlie make-up (which he applied himself) and I thought that he looked better than a lot of actual girls of that era!

They rehearsed for the *Pyromania* tour and the first show was early February 1983 at the Marquee in Wardour Street, Soho, in London's West End. A small venue (capacity 1,000) but a prestigious venue in those days.

I was stationed at stage right, taking care of Steve and Sav. Not much room. Phil had lots of room on stage left and he ruled the space afforded to him.

In the dressing room, a tiny space, not suitable for any band that could actually fill the place, I watched Phil Collen for the first time, looking at himself in a cracked mirror, throwing his body poses, and honing his chops. I remember thinking that this guy is nothing like I have ever seen in preparation prior to a show. He shaped and postured and made faces to himself, not caring who might have been watching. He just practised his skill, just like an athlete, training and perfecting his ability to appeal to his potential fans. At that point, I realized that he was just like top-class athletes prior to running the hundred yards or vaulting the horse in order to make it a perfect ten!

The show went really well.

After that, I soon observed him practising his guitar while sitting on the toilet. Whenever he went for a crap, he took a guitar with him. He could be heard from outside chopping and shredding on an electric guitar, taking way more time than the average guy taking a shit.

As Malvin recounts, before anything got under way Def Leppard booked a warm-up show of sorts at my old stomping ground, the Marquee Club in London. This was to be my first live appearance with the band, and I couldn't think of a better venue. We would be premiering some tracks off *Pyromania*, but most importantly, we'd be giving the fans a look at this new version of Def Leppard.

There had been a lot of chatter in the press when I joined the band, and I was anxious to answer any concerns people might have about me being too flamboyant or too glam. Fans and critics can get so used to a line-up that whenever there is some monumental shift, it's up to the new guy to really prove he belongs. So it's that much more important for a band to play live. No matter how much you play in the studio or how much you rehearse, there's nothing like getting in front of people. One person in a room can make a difference because all of a sudden you start playing to that person. That's what performers do. So I was very anxious and excited to get things under way. The band was in a great mood that night and the club was packed. Not just with fans but with a lot of musicians who were curious about the new look of the band and the sound of the new record. There was a lot of anticipation about Def Leppard at this moment.

Once we hit the stage, I felt like I'd been playing with these guys my whole life. The chemistry, the timing and the camaraderie were so natural and effortless. Especially between Steve and me onstage, there seemed to be something really magical. By this point I think we had truly started to bond as a live band, and it showed onstage. This was an amazing way to kick off.

It was a lot of fun ending with 'Travelin' Band'. That

classic Creedence Clearwater Revival song became part of our repertoire for the whole tour, and we extended the tune into a vamped-up nine-minute jam that featured some wild solos and even bits of other songs like Zeppelin's 'Rock and Roll'. Years later Joe and I heard a Def Leppard bootleg and had completely forgotten that Brian Robertson of Thin Lizzy had joined us onstage for the encore shindig. That night, we broke through all the expectations about me and about the band's new material. Everyone was impressed, as critic Justine Cole reflected in *Sounds*:

*New material from 'Pyromania' came over well, the highlights being 'Rock of Ages' – an absolute stormer of a number . . . Phil Collen, whose gutsy style proves that he's more than just a pretty boy as many had feared. Leppard 1983-style are flash, brash and have all the pride of their leonine namesakes. Quite simply, Def Leppard have come of age and look set to confound their critics with no small degree of style.*

Dave Ling at *Classic Rock* reported:

*Those who feared that new recruit Phil Collen, formerly of mascara-glad glamsters Girl, would be a pretty boy fill-in for the shandied-up ex-guitarist Pete Willis were in for a pleasant surprise. Got up in natty looking string vest, Collen let rip with gritty lead runs and stinging solos, quickly winning the crowd over and forming an effective partnership with the grinning Steve 'Steamin" Clark.*

And so we were off. We had been released from the cage, fired from the gun, however you want to look at it. The next era of Def Leppard had begun. We felt strong and confident. The roller-coaster ride, the Def Leppard juggernaut, had officially taken off.

*Pyromania* was strong out of the gate. It hit No. 16 on the *Billboard* album chart in just a month. Two weeks later it was in the top ten. Sales were strong in America, and the reviews continued to pour in.

'*Hit Parader* readers will recognize this as the real thing. Def Leppard's *Pyromania* is a tribute to what a producer's art heavy metal has become. Mutt (AC/DC, Foreigner) Lange provides young Leppard with layers upon layers of sound until solid waves drown out all but the jagged edges of Phil Collen, Steve Clark and ex-member Pete Willis on guitar and Joe Elliott's high-pitched vocals.'

Given how well our debut club show was received, and how well our album was reviewed and was selling in the States, what followed soon after was a bit of a letdown. It was as if people were unaware we had even released a record. Two days after the gig at the Marquee Club, we crammed into our band bus and headed to Ireland, where we played another warm-up gig at the TV Club in Dublin. It was poorly attended. Then on 12 February, the *Pyromania* tour officially began at Belfast's Ulster Hall, in Northern Ireland. Again, the place was probably half-empty. What the fuck?

The other thing that was pretty obvious was that we would be given a hard time by the British press about 'selling out' to America. This is where I developed an opinion that I still maintain to this day. That is that you should play where people want to see you. With the release of *Pyromania*, the way that we sounded was ravenously devoured in the United States. So it seemed like a no-brainer that most of the time would be spent where this album was being played continuously on the radio and on MTV. To this day, we are larger in America than we have ever been in our home country. If we were the biggest band in Lithuania, then I would suggest we spend more time there.

So we continued the tour going through Europe. Although we were playing small and not overly attended venues, it was thrilling to be a part of this band performing the mainly unheard of *Pyromania* to these audiences. You could easily tour through places in Europe back then. For some reason, today it's dried up. But back then there was a thriving rock scene for us.

Though we all shared one bus with our managers and crew members, when it came to staying in hotels, the rooming situations broke down like this: Joe and Sav were roommates; Rick Allen roomed with his brother, Robert, who was also the road manager; and Steve Clark and I shared a room.

Even though Steve and I had known each other for a few years, when we lived together on tour we quickly became best friends. It wasn't just the guitar playing or extreme boozing – we both found that we were soaking up all that we could and learning more on the road than we had ever learned at school, with a healthy appetite for new and exciting cultural discoveries. We also found that we loved each other's company. We could get into deep conversations that would last for hours.

It was also on this tour that Phil Wilkie, our stage monitor engineer, came up with the term 'the Terror Twins' for Steve and me. As I vaguely remember it, we had invited Phil out with us for an evening of drinking on one of our off nights on the tour, but he said to us, 'I ain't going out with you two – the Terror Twins.' And so the legend was born. Needless to say, Steve and I got into countless episodes of skullduggery and mayhem. Unfortunately, I was drinking at the time, so my memory serves no purpose here. You'll probably be better off Googling our antics and telling me about them. If we've offended anyone, I sincerely apologize.

Both our lives were changing in massive ways, and we were going through it together, like brothers. We cracked up watching *Spinal Tap* together after Spandau Ballet made us watch it. We talked about our childhoods. We explored places like Paris and Munich, soaking up as much culture as we could. And we tried to make sense of the fact that the lives we'd known were now fading as we sailed toward something much bigger and unknown. We also explored where we could go with our music.

One day Steve said to me, 'Phil, I've always felt this thing. Jimmy Page kind of does it, and Brian May kind of does it, but instead of doing harmony guitars like Thin Lizzy or the Allman Brothers, what if we did a more orchestral approach together, meshing our guitars together in a whole new way? Almost like keyboards might interact.' And that would eventually become the Def Leppard sound an album later. Like I said, Steve was just such a different kind of player. Honestly, he was. Totally unique and unencumbered by rules or anything. He was a lot like Jimmy Page, in my opinion. Page would have these ideas that were very orchestral; it really defined his sound. He used very complicated themes, and exotic textures and melodies.

By March, the European part of the tour had just a couple of weeks left, and so we made our way through France and Switzerland, and played a few more shows in England before our last show on 15 March in Melun, France, at the Salle des Fêtes.

Then we had a couple of days off before boarding a plane and heading over to the States, where we would join the Billy Squier tour as the opening act in Atlanta on 18 March. Billy Squier was touring his second album. All the success of the first album and notably of the song 'The Stroke' was culminating with this tour. We would work our way up the East Coast, playing in Charlotte, North Carolina, all the way up to Portland, Maine, and then back down to Connecticut and Long Island, with a big show at Nassau Coliseum.

Def Leppard already had a couple of American tours under their belt, opening for bands such as Ozzy Osbourne and the Scorpions, among others. But for me this was my first trip to the States since my cross-country Greyhound bus tour several years earlier. I was ecstatic to be going back.

We'd heard rumours that *Pyromania* was off to a decent start in the States and that the first single, 'Photograph', was starting to get a bit of airplay. That said, we were the opening act and so we didn't have much of an idea of what to expect. I was excited, I think, mainly because of the American audience. Returning to this mythical place was almost surreal for me.

Each night, we noticed the crowds getting bigger and arriving earlier – they were coming to see us. We also started noticing that they really seemed to know the new music, too. That meant they were not just listening to the radio. They were watching their MTV. The videos had been a hit. We also couldn't ignore the fact that each night we were outselling Billy Squier at the merchandise tables. It wasn't even close. A lot of that had to do with the Union Jack insignias that were on our T-shirts, inspired, of course, by the Union Jack clothing that Rick and Joe wore in those first two videos. The Union Jack got a jolt of life because of our videos, and American teens were suddenly adopting the look.

City by city, the enthusiasm for Def Leppard was growing.

So much so, we nearly forgot that we were the opening act, given how full the arenas were when we took the stage – a fact that was hard to ignore in Chicago. Def Leppard had not played Chicago since the *High 'n' Dry* tour, back in 1981. That night at the UIC Pavilion we went out and played our usual set and noticed that the arena was packed, much like it had been in recent venues. But tonight it seemed like the whole audience was there to see Def Leppard. At the end of our set, many of the kids actually *left*. And it hit us: they had come to see *our band*.

For the next two weeks, we played all throughout the Midwest, hitting Indianapolis; Cincinnati; Lexington, Kentucky; and Kansas City. We went down to New Mexico and up to Minnesota. And each night was more and more exciting for us.

At the start of the tour, Michael Jackson's *Thriller* all but owned the charts. The singles 'Billie Jean', 'Beat It' and the title track were all in heavy rotation across the States, competing with other big radio hits by the Police, Billy Idol and Prince, among others. In May 1983, *Pyromania* would go on to become No. 2 on the charts, behind *Thriller*, and it stayed there for about six months.

That was mind-blowing to us, but we never really stopped to bask in the glow of anything. We were a very working-class band – we just concentrated on playing our best. We never took anything for granted. And for all the drinking we did on the road, we remained amazingly disciplined when it came to playing. We actually had a rule that no matter what went on offstage, no one went onstage drunk. It simply would not happen. We were always very serious about the music part of it. We felt we owed too much to ourselves and to our fans, who had forked out considerable money to see their favourite band. After all, this was a dream come true. Why would you fuck it up? We drank plenty after the show. There was always time for that. But the shows were sacred.

By April, we learned that plans were being put in place for Def Leppard to embark on their first-ever headlining US tour, which would start the next month. We were thrilled. America was falling in love with us and the record was approaching gold status. It seemed that the British rock press went the other way, slagging us for selling out to America and being too polished. But that was OK, as *Pyromania* was becoming huge in the United States. So it seemed obvious that we would do the lion's share of our touring there.

We wrapped up the Billy Squier tour with shows all along the West Coast and then, on an off day, we went and taped an episode of *American Bandstand* with Dick Clark. It didn't really hit me then how important that was, given that I had been weaned on shows like *The Old Grey Whistle Test*. But it really was an important TV appearance for us in America. *Pyromania* was officially on fire.

It was the perfect recipe at the perfect time. Culturally, it seemed, we had the look and the songs – the perfect hybrid of pop and hard rock – that hit a nerve with young American fans. For all of the upbeat pop on the radio, there was really no one else like us at that point, and I think that's why we stood out so much with *Pyromania*. Radio programmers appreciated how accessible our songs were, while we still maintained the integrity of a hard-rock band.

Steve and I both knew something was happening when, one night in a Midwestern hotel restaurant, some fans saw us and went crazy; we both had to be escorted out to the kitchen. That had never happened to either of us before. We just looked at each other and laughed. There was something almost absurd about it. Like the old black-and-white newsreels of the Beatles in public with all the girls crying and fainting. That's the night that I think we first felt the full force of the MTV effect. Girls were falling in love with us, and guys thought we 'rocked, dude'. So it was really a win-win.

It was stunning to us that things could change so quickly. We were about to get swept up in a mania that I don't think any of us had ever imagined for Def Leppard. Sure, we had always wished for that sort of thing, but, knowing how hard it was to achieve, for us, it was just a fantasy. The thought of making it always seemed to be on the local level. Like, you'd play and get recognized locally in the street and be able to fill your local cinema-type theatre. I don't think any of us thought about how far-reaching our success would be.

We also didn't think about how big geographically America was.

We would get crazed pop star attention, something we never thought could exist for a rock band. For example, when we played a charity soccer game in Omaha, more than 10,000 people showed up. We had to stop doing record in-stores after an incident in Denver involving a collapsed platform and 3,000 people who were trying to enter the store where we were signing autographs. The other interesting thing we learned about was the boundaries otherwise normal people would remove for themselves.

Especially American girls. When we toured the States, we learned a hell of a lot more about what some girls would do to gain access. When we arrived at one gig, we saw a huge line of girls outside the venue. They were actually waiting to go down on crew members just to get to us. They wanted to give head all the time – almost as if we were doing them a favour instead of them performing one. For instance, during our first US headlining tour, I was waiting for an elevator in a hotel. A really hot girl who I had never seen in my life came up to me, pulled my pants down and went down on me, and didn't say a word. This type of stuff didn't happen before with total strangers. So you assess the psychology of the situation. There were girls in the night-time, different girls in the daytime, and different ones the next night.

I didn't chase women or adventure. Both seemed to find

me. My conclusion was not to take all the fame stuff too seriously, as the reasons for this type of behaviour are quite superficial, as great as it was. Eventually we created a back-stage pass known as a 'boiler pass'. It was given to any girl who had done this favour to get backstage. Instead of saying *Def Leppard*, the pass said *Dik Likker* in the band's logo font. At first glance it looked like a regular Def Leppard backstage pass. But you had to look closely for the wording and the smiley face to differentiate official guests from extreme groupies.

The other really interesting thing about this kind of fame is that it isn't sustainable. We were to have bigger albums later in our career and more attention. But this type of pop frenzy seems more exciting and over-the-top when a band or artist first explodes onto the scene. It was always different after the *Pyromania* tour. The next album, *Hysteria*, had a different dynamic – but we'll get to that later.

On 21 April 1983, we did one last opening gig for Billy Squier, in Portland, Oregon, then headed to Texas, where we would have a week or so to get ready for our first head-lining tour, which we would take very seriously. What I've noticed over the years, especially with other touring bands, is that a lot of them seem to think that being on tour is just an excuse to act out a lot of these crazy stories that provide fuel and fodder for future anecdotes. It's almost like it's some giant frat party. We never really fell into that. Yeah, we've got some crazy stories, but we were always more serious about the music we made and about being a great live band. We were young, but our music always took precedence over the shenanigans.

We would also now have our own opening acts for the tour, and those would include the Jon Butcher Axis, Krokus, Gary Moore (from Thin Lizzy) and eventually Uriah Heep. Let me talk about Gary Moore for a moment. Gary's guitar playing was a huge influence on me. His vibrato and technique were astonishing, so when I found myself back-stage jamming with Gary, I stayed there as long as I could. In fact, probably for over an hour, because I got a blister on my finger from extreme shredding. Gary let me play his classic and very famous Gibson Les Paul that had belonged to Fleetwood Mac's Peter Green. Gary was also using heavier strings than me – hence the blister. But the experience also influenced me to use heavier-gauge strings, because you could play way more aggressively and the guitar would stay in tune.

One fascinating thing we noticed as we set off through Texas, Oklahoma, Louisiana and Mississippi was that the size of our crowds could almost be measured directly depending on whether or not these cities and towns were already wired for cable television.

I know it sounds strange, but places that had cable TV had MTV, and places that had MTV had us *all the time*. That was the part we were sort of disconnected from. We were becoming bigger than life as a band in all of these key places that happened to have cable. So by the time we came to town, we'd already become rock gods to these kids in places like Norman, Oklahoma, and Monroe, Louisiana, that didn't always have big bands rolling through. I just can't state strongly enough how important MTV was to Def Leppard. As all of the previous bands we'd looked up to shied away from being presented in such a commercial medium, we took it in our stride. We were young and pretty, but we were a hard-rock band. That paradox made us hugely successful. We were slotted in seamlessly next to artists like Michael Jackson, Billy Idol, U2 and INXS. But, as I stated before, this kind of fame isn't sustainable. When formats change along with how people perceive and get their music, everything else is affected. This was all brand new for us. We were in the perfect place at the right time. When this leg of the tour started, *Pyromania* had really begun to go to the next level. In just a few weeks it would be selling 100,000 copies a week for pretty much the rest of the year.

As we continued our trek across America, we started developing other rules of the road. A big one was that nobody was allowed to bring girls on the bus. Ever. We had really started bonding as a group and were very protective of each other and our space. There were plenty of bands that always had their bus jam-packed with chicks, but our thing was different. We hadn't started a band to 'get chicks',

Jane.

Tarzan.

Ken and Connie's wedding.

Mum and Dad with some weird-looking baby.

Me and my dad at 223 Boundary Road in the late fifties.

I fell off this apple tree a few years later and tore a bloody hole in my groin.

Me in a pram.

Me and Nan.

I still have this guitar in London. I didn't start playing until I was sixteen.

I have no idea why I am
holding this monkey.

Pocket pool.

Flexing my abs at Jaywick On Sea.

Me getting older in the back garden at Boundary Road.

My dad's van. Many an adventure and holiday was had in this Austin van.

My dog Coffee and a couple of invincible superheroes in the back garden at Boundary Road.

The swim team. Front row, right to left: my buddy David Cole; me; and my swim coach, Giles Brown.

Martin Blackman and me at fourteen.

My mum's oldest sister,
Dorothy. We're still in touch.
She's ninety-three now.

Warick Boys football team. The boy holding the ball next to me in the front row is Chris Green.
Whenever we had sporting events at other schools, they thought we were cheating by using a grown
man, but we were actually the same age.

My first appearance at the Marquee Club in London with Lucy. I was seventeen.

Jeff Hepting (left) and me at a Dumb Blonds gig.

**Me jamming with Ritchie Blackmore at the Marquee Club in London. How fucking cool is that?**

**Me and my mum. Pyromania tour, California, 1983.**

Left to right: Steve's mum, Beryl; Rick Allen's mum, Kath; me; and my mum.

Me and Steve. Contrary to popular belief, not a couple.

as so many guys liked to say back then. We genuinely all shared the idea that we were in a band to make music. The 'roadie mentality', which we didn't allow, was that you just live for the moment, don't care who is on your bus, just go for the quick kill. We were wired differently. We took it all a bit more seriously and really did put the music first. We didn't want any strangers infiltrating our little bubble. Of course, if one of our girlfriends came to visit and travel with us for a week or two, that was fine. But no strangers were allowed, especially on the bus.

We were also lucky to have the managers that we did because it would have been very easy at that time to throw money away like so many bands were doing. Our managers at the time were still Peter Mensch and Cliff Burnstein. They were the ultimate 'good-cop/bad-cop' duo. Cliff was hyper-intelligent, very softly-spoken and always on point. Peter would roar like a lion at anyone who was trying to take advantage of us, even getting people fired from our record label. We were so fortunate to have this team in place, especially at this time when musical formats were about to change. One of the greatest things Peter and Cliff did for us was make sure that if a new format of music ever came on to the market, the record label would have to get Def Leppard's permission before they released music on that particular format. Peter and Cliff obviously saw into the future and realized that cassettes would be long gone when CDs emerged and that ultimately digital formats would change the music industry forever. Record labels did not adjust artist royalties accordingly for the release of their music on digital media even though their overheads (i.e. the cost to produce hard copy music) became almost non-existent. This is why to date a lot of original Def Leppard music is not on iTunes, etc. Many artists would be completely ripped off because they did not have the Mensch-Burnstein clause in their contract. We were lucky.

Mensch also kept expenses in line – and our heads on straight when it came to finances. Early on in the tour we would take limos to and from hotels and venues, thinking we were pretty cool. Mensch soon pointed out the ridiculousness of this perk, saying, 'You know how much those things cost?' No, we didn't. But here's the true break-down that Mensch would do for us on paper: Limos (two-hour minimum). Two cars to get to the venue and two cars to get back to the hotel. The hotel run was after midnight – an extra charge. At four or five shows a week, we realized that was about $10,000. We all looked at each other and said, 'Why not save that money for something we really want to do? Why throw it away on a limo when there is a hotel van that will take us to the gig for free?' We all heard many stories of bands blowing money on any-thing and everything. Not us. Coming from mostly nothing, we didn't want to waste anything. So right away we became very different to a lot of the other bands out there who were being very destructive and blowing tons of money while destroying hotel rooms and living out of limousines.

In June of 1983 we reconnected with our music video director David Mallet. He met us at a place called the Ritz Theatre in Elizabeth, New Jersey, where we recorded our third video from the *Pyromania* album, for 'Foolin''. It entered the heavy rotation of MTV in August and was played into the ground as much as 'Photograph' and 'Rock of Ages'.

We got back on tour and hit Fort Myers, Florida, where my hotel room was broken into and everything was stolen – all of my clothes, everything. The hotel was a motel-type number with direct access to the beach. I'd just come back from a stroll wearing only shorts, a T-shirt and flip-flops. This was the first real hassle I experienced on what was otherwise the greatest tour I'd ever been on in my life. But I was saved by a group of local teenagers in the next town, which was Hampton, Virginia. This included a young lady who we now know as Doctor Dot, a brilliant masseuse who runs a successful chiropractic and massage empire. I told them what had happened, and they took me to a nearby army/navy surplus store where they bought their clothes. I got loaded up with a bunch of camouflage clothing, and that's what I wore for the balance of the American tour. If you see photos of me from that period, that's why I am suddenly wearing camo onstage. And similar to the Union Jack clothing, the camo look started to catch on as a result. A week later, the police contacted me with news that they had found some of my stuff (they probably saw a homeless guy wandering aimlessly in my blue silk blouse and tight white pants), but I already had a new look.

The tour rolled on and, as we hit the West Coast in mid-September, we surprised our families and flew all of our parents out to travel with us down the coast from San Francisco for two big gigs at the Forum in Los Angeles. We were all homesick and decided, 'Why not bring home to us?' This was the first time any of our parents had ever been to America. (My mum came but my dad couldn't make it.) We had a great time travelling with them on our bus and letting them see exactly what we did for a living. They got to watch us perform in a couple of magnificent venues and had a chance to see the insane crowds. This was the first time they got to see all of their 'little boys' as full-blown rock stars, and they all had a blast.

By the time we got to the Forum, there was another treat in store for us. Queen guitarist Brian May had always been a source of inspiration for us. He had been sort of tracking our success. So on the second night we played at the Forum, on 11 September, Brian agreed to come join us on the encore 'Travelin' Band'.

Having Brian May come out meant the world to us. I'd seen Queen go from an opening act in England to becoming this megaforce in music. Def Leppard always based its sound on a hybrid of Queen-meets-AC/DC. I was amazed at how humble and nice Brian was, being that he was also this monster talent. It wasn't just his guitar playing – it was the melodies, the vocals, the songwriting. I've always thought Brian was underrated. He was the ultimate team player, always putting the band and the song before his own ego. None of that takes away from his guitar playing, but in fact you focus in on the music as opposed to the individual. People ask, 'What's important about being in a band?' Brian May sums it right up.

Much like the night I jammed with Ritchie Blackmore, the night Brian May stepped out onstage with us was a revelation. To hear those incredible sounds coming out of his guitar while we played right next to him was a thrill, especially for Sav. To this day, Queen is Rick Savage's favourite band. I still hear their influence in his songwriting and his approach to music. To say Sav freaked out is putting it mildly.

It was hard to believe that a tour that had begun at the tiny Marquee Club in London was about to come to a close in a sold-out baseball stadium with more than 60,000 rabid fans. It was Saturday, 17 September. We'd come through San Diego earlier that year, in April, opening up for Billy Squier. But it was hard to fathom what had happened since then. The concert, put on by local radio station KGB, was billed as 'Sky Show VIII', and the end would feature one of the biggest fireworks shows in history. And Mötley Crüe, Uriah Heep and Eddie Money would be opening for *us*.

When our bus pulled up early that morning and we first walked into Jack Murphy Stadium, I'll have to admit we were a bit awestruck. We were just wearing cut-off shorts and flip-flops, wandering around this massive venue trying to make sense of it all. It almost didn't matter that our album was burning up the airwaves or that the tour was selling out faster than shows by Michael Jackson. This truly felt like the big time, like we had really arrived.

We would never have to explain to our parents again exactly what we did and why we did it. They were right there to experience it with us onstage and under the lights, and they went home with a million and one stories to tell their friends.

This extraordinary tour of America ended with two shows in Honolulu. It was a great chance for us to catch our breath, spend some time on the beach and think about what the last couple of months had been like.

As we wound down, *Pyromania* was still No. 2 on the album charts, right behind Michael Jackson's *Thriller*, where it would remain for months, on its way to selling ten million copies. 'Photograph' had reached No. 1 on the *Billboard* Mainstream Rock Chart and 'Rock of Ages' hit No. 1 on the *Billboard* Top Tracks Chart. There were radio stations that would play the entire album beginning to end. We heard about fans burning through multiple copies. And it seemed you couldn't turn dials without hitting one rock station that was cranking one of our songs. Def Leppard went from being basically a hard-rock radio filler band to Top 40 superstars.

Def Leppard's first two albums, *High 'n' Dry* and *On Through the Night*, had barely cracked the Top 40 and just missed the Top 50, respectively. We had experienced something monumental and unforgettable on this tour of the States, and *Pyromania* truly became a defining moment in the band's history.

Our lives had changed, that was true, but another thing was also true. I was drinking more. On the road and playing, there was temptation everywhere. We were surrounded by people who wanted to take us to dinner or throw us parties – both environments that encouraged drinking. Steve and I were drinking so much that there were certain days I could not remember. One time in France our road manager, Robert Allen, came by our hotel room with our shoes after a night of I don't know what. 'You two were out of control last night,' he said as he sat down. Apparently, Steve and I, after pulling our trousers off in a bar, had bought drinks for everyone. Then, Robert told us, 'You and Steve had a fight in an elevator. You threw up in someone's Mercedes. There were these chicks involved. It was a fucking mess.' Steve and I just looked at each other. We both remembered nothing.

And it would only get worse.

In September 1983, Joe and I travelled to Tokyo to do some promotion and set the stage for when Def Leppard would visit there in January. Even though the promoters had us booked wall-to-wall, doing more than a dozen interviews per day, we still managed to have a really good time. John and Roger Taylor from Duran Duran were staying at the same hotel, so we hung with them for a bit while soaking up the Japanese culture. Those guys had been there before and knew all the best clubs. They took Joe and me around, and one night, in our drunken revelry, Joe announced, 'We're going to form a supergroup! Def Leppard and Duran Duran, the four of us!' Sounded like a great idea when we were all bolloxed drunk.

The trip was short, so it seemed like no time at all before we were back on a plane returning to Stockholm to meet up with the band to start our European tour. Now, this may not seem like a big deal to you, but it was on this flight that I made a big decision: it was the last time I ate meat. I remember leaning over to Joe and saying, 'I can't eat this any more.' I'd been toying with the idea of removing meat from my diet for a while, but this time I was serious about becoming a vegetarian. The reasons were multiple and had been growing for years. My grandmother once left me a steak to grill that was bleeding and full of veins. I was sixteen and disgusted. I don't think I ate it. After seeing the original *Texas Chainsaw Massacre* and the reality of how barbaric the slaughter/torture process is, I just couldn't justify trying to satisfy my palate with something that had to die when it was just as easy to eat something that didn't have to suffer.

My ego isn't that big. My decision wasn't so well received at first. Back in the eighties, vegetarianism was not as popular (dare I say trendy) as it is today. People made fun of me. It's a bit like when you're trying not to drink. But once I made the decision and stuck with it, I felt extremely empowered and relieved. I genuinely didn't give a fuck about what anyone else thought and entered a different part of my life based on being very secure in the decision I'd made. I'm still very secure in that decision. In fact, at the time of writing, I've transitioned to veganism. For those who don't know (because I get this question all the time), a vegan is a vegetarian who doesn't eat any animal products or by-products. This includes dairy, eggs and honey.

That I stopped eating fish didn't mean I stopped drinking like one. Once Joe and I arrived at our hotel to meet up with the rest of the band, Steve and I decided to head down to the hotel bar for a few drinks with the road crew. We were all still sporting our tans from the American tour, and Steve and I were wearing shorts and flip-flops. I'll admit, Steve and I were being a bit obnoxious, flaunting ourselves out on the dance floor and showing off until finally this big Swedish guy at the bar got a little bit pissed off. Some beer got spilled on the dance floor and all of a sudden everybody started slipping and sliding around. Before you know it, we've got what looks like a Wild West saloon brawl on our hands. It was straight out of a classic Western movie. Chairs, tables and glasses were flying all over the place, with punches being thrown left and right. I kicked at the Swedish guy after he decked me with a punch, but my flip-flop flew off and I wound up with a huge gash in the sole of my foot from the broken glass all over the floor.

It was absolutely insane. One of our road crew guys, a massive gent, levelled the Swedish guy with a couple of solid punches before getting himself thrown through a plate-glass window. The crew, who were all drunk off their asses, were all pulling shards of broken glass out of the bottom of my foot. They used vodka as an anaesthetic.

The next day, when we checked out, Steve and I had to pay for everything (rightly so). For about two weeks I could hardly walk on that foot, and my ankle was numb for at least six months. It really cramped my stage performances. It was a lesson learned. But the irony of my new healthy diet alongside my unhealthy drinking hadn't quite hit home yet. Not that my abandonment of flesh eating had anything to do with health.

*Pyromania* was still selling 100,000 copies a week in the United States, but you wouldn't have known it in Europe. The album had not caught fire in other parts of the world as it had in America, so there we were, back to slogging it out just as we'd been doing several months before. It was weird and, I gotta admit, slightly depressing to go within just a few weeks from playing to crowds that numbered between 20,000 and 50,000 per night to playing half-empty clubs. And the local press derided us, as they had when the record started to take off in America. Again, they implied that we had somehow 'sold out'. It was the strangest thing. It brought us down a bit, but we were starting to understand the drill. Things were just different in America. Thankfully, though, the three English shows all sold out and we played a fantastic gig on 5 December at the Hammersmith Odeon. We had a big end-of-tour party afterward, with Billy Gibbons of ZZ Top joining us, along with some friends from Motörhead and Iron Maiden, and our families.

Being back home was kind of weird, too. I was living back at my mum's and things were sort of like the old days. There was a lot going on in our lives during this time. We had left home, been on tour for a year and, without realizing it, had cut our mothers' apron strings. This was a big deal, considering we were all pretty much mummy's boys. We went from living in working-class, family-oriented English neighbourhoods to spinning around the world and settling into expensive, exotic cities. And now it was time to start shaping our own lives away from home.

Everyone's life in the neighbourhood was basically the same. I had a new Porsche, but that was really the only thing I splurged on. When I was younger, I'd driven an old beat-up Ford Cortina. When *Pyromania* blew up, I replaced my old Ford Cortina with a black Porsche, and within a week of my owning this car, a beautiful South African model knocked on my window as I was sitting in traffic on Blackfriars Bridge in London and gave me her number. Funny, that never happened in my Ford Cortina.

That's how it was for all of us. We had been treated like rock stars while on tour, but now we were all just home, where we had started. But we did have money. I was now making more in one week than I had in the previous year. And with that came some new realities.

One day during a band meeting, one of our managers said to us, 'Boys, the good news is you're making a lot of money. The bad news, at least in the UK, is you're making a lot of money.' We all knew what he was talking about.

Being British citizens who for the first time in our lives actually made some money, we were now subject to the British tax system. Back then Britain demanded a very high tax rate to be paid by people earning money in the top percentage bracket. We'd heard horror stories about celebrities being taxed 90 per cent on the pound. That means that for every pound they made, 90 per cent (90p) went to the British government. By the time we arrived back home, the top tax rate was about 60 per cent. However, many top earners took advantage of a tax loophole: they became tax exiles. They moved out of the country. The law stated that if you spent fewer than sixty-two days in England you weren't liable to pay those taxes. In the seventies, Rod Stewart famously released an album called *Atlantic Crossing* and that's exactly what he did to escape this taxation. The Rolling Stones all moved out in the early 1970s for the same reason after playing a famous 'farewell' tour of their homeland.

We were advised to become tax exiles. It made sense, as we were spending more and more time out of the country anyway: none of us came from money, and who knew how long our success would last? So we did. We all chose different countries to live in. Joe and Sav up and left for Dublin, Ireland, since they really wanted to be somewhere that was similar to a British culture (Heinz Baked Beans, live football on TV, etc.) and Rick Allen went to Amsterdam. Steve and I went off to Paris. Unbeknownst to us, it was the start of a spiritual and intellectual quest.

At the end of 1983, I went to a Christmas party in London with Peter Mensch and Sue, his fiancée at the time, at pop singer and Visage front man Steve Strange's house. We had a lovely Christmas dinner. Among the guests were Ronnie Wood, Boy George and Lorelei Shellist, who was a friend of Peter's. Lorelei was an American model who lived in Paris with her friend, another model, Valerie Mazzonelli. When I mentioned to Lorelei that Steve and I would be spending some time in Paris, she suggested that when we got there we give her a call and they'd show us around.

Before I actually called Lorelei, an incident happened one night in January 1984 after going out with Steve, Monique – a girl I was seeing – and my mum, who'd come over for the weekend. While we were out in Paris, a car zoomed around the corner, hitting Monique and sending her flying. The car then went to drive off. So I kicked it as it drove away. It stopped. Five guys jumped out. A brawl ensued. My mum was freaking out. Monique came into the fight and one of the guys punched her in the face. So we all just got into it. I think Steve and I came out the worst, with chipped teeth and black eyes. When we met up with Peter Mensch and the rest of the guys at Heathrow airport a few days later to embark on our first tour of Australia, we didn't want them to know how much we had been tearing it up, so we got stewardesses on the flight over to put make-up on us. But as soon as we saw everyone, they enquired, 'Have you guys been fighting?'

We left to perform at the Narara Festival, a three-day event in New South Wales, on the east coast of Australia. This was the band's very first time down under, and we loved every minute of it. And I got to see my cousin Georgie, who'd emigrated to Oz from Wales years earlier.

The show that we had gone down for took place in late January and also featured Simple Minds, the Pretenders, Talking Heads and the Eurythmics – the quintessential eighties pop line-up. The weather was foreboding all day, with off-and-on bursts of rain. But our set occurred during the most torrential, biblical rainstorm I'd ever seen. Nearly all of the 35,000 audience members left. There were 3,000 die-hards waiting. We certainly hadn't come all the way down to Australia to not play due to the weather, even though it was extreme, plus those who were left in the mud deserved our best and wettest performance. Since most of the other bands had bailed due to the weather, the fans really seemed to appreciate us hanging in there and playing for them. We were not really that well known in Australia, and so it was our first big impression. To this day we meet fans who were there on that very wet day in 1984 and they still thank us profusely for not leaving the show. Our legend had begun to take root in Oz.

# 3

Although by now we'd travelled around the world and had even played in France, Steve and I had never really been exposed to a place like Paris for any length of time. The city is one of the most gorgeous and romantic in the world, rich with architecture, culture and history. When you live there, it's a whole different ball game. So much so I began noticing architectural and structural beauty when I'd go back to England – something I had never noticed the whole time I was growing up.

The museums, galleries, cafés and clubs we went to affected our view on so many things, especially coming from such humble working-class surroundings. Steve and I took to having very deep philosophical discussions. We literally stumbled upon awareness. Apart from becoming avid book readers, we started comparing notes on life based on our childhoods, parents, the psychology of past, present and future girlfriends, and humans in general. There's a term known as 'the dumbing down of America', which refers to the steps taken to make it easier to control the herd. This refers to keeping the masses docile via reality TV, sports and entertainment. To put it bluntly, there's a quest to impair logical thought process, comprehensive reasoning and responsible decision making by taking people's eyes off the ball. This happens everywhere, not just in America. Once Steve and I realized this, it changed everything, as if we were stepping into a third dimension. We could never look at life the same again.

During this time we even applied our newfound logic to our musical selves. Steve and I would sometimes speak for hours nonstop about everything. We were like sponges. We took everything in. This even made us think 'outside the box' about the role of guitars in a rock band. We approached music differently. We didn't just want to be standard. Instead of being these guitars that were just thundering along, we wanted to create orchestral sounds while retaining the groove and melody of a credible rock band.

Some of my friends and family members couldn't under-stand the cultural growth I experienced in Paris. Being raised in a very structured working-class environment, we didn't really grow up talking about art and architecture; my new interests were received as pretension. Steve was also having the same issues. Since he was from Sheffield, it was even more of an extreme contrast. But we didn't care. We were ready to break away a bit and explore the opportunities that were presenting themselves as a result of our success.

We also had other, less intellectual reasons to like Paris: Valerie and Lorelei. Shortly after Steve and I moved to Paris I started seeing Valerie and Steve started dating Lorelei. Liz and I had drifted apart by this point. She'd never really be out of my life, but in terms of a relationship, we had moved on . . . for now. Initially, Steve and I stayed at Lorelei and Valerie's place on the rue Budé, Isle St Louis, a tiny island on the River Seine next to Notre Dame Cathedral. The apartment looked like it was created for a Gothic film set, the building being hundreds of years old. The four of us would rent a car and take road trips to places like ancient Deauville, in Normandy, where we would end up sleeping in the car because all the hotels were booked. We attended a few of the girls' modelling events, and I would eventually buy my first apartment, a place that Valerie found, around Boulevard St Germain in the Sixth Arrondissement. Steve stayed with Lorelei in her apartment on the Isle St Louis. I have wonderful memories about my place in Paris. There was a great Italian restaurant opposite my second-floor apartment. Valerie and I would order food; then the waiter would whistle up from the street when it was ready. My Paris experience was actually happening in segments taking place while we were writing and recording the *Hysteria* album in Dublin and Holland. I was going back and forth but was in Paris when I learned about Rick's accident.

After well-deserved downtime following the craziness that was the *Pyromania* tour, we were all anxious to get back with Mutt to discuss the direction of the band and begin work on the next album. In February 1984 we all convened in Dublin, where we set up camp for about six months to write before going off to Holland to record. The pressure was on for us to follow *Pyro*'s success.

We found a house to rent on St Helen's Road, Booterstown, overlooking the Irish Sea. We drew straws as to who would get which room. Sav got a room where the heater wouldn't turn off for the whole six months we were there. When it came to choosing my room, I chose the one with the sea view. Unfortunately, it was the tiniest box room in the house. Joe, however, had a view of Mount Kilimanjaro and the hanging gardens of Babylon from his room. Ironically, this straw-drawing technique was employed for the next three houses. Joe always seemed to get the biggest room wherever we stayed. I was convinced he rigged the straws somehow. We all lived under one roof – five guys who'd practically lived with their parents their whole lives, living in a house together. You do the math. If you needed a plate, you'd pull it out of the pile in the sink, wash it, use it and put it back for the next starving victim. There was an airing cupboard upstairs to dry out towels and sheets and stuff, but we used it for brewing homemade beer. Our local pub was called the Punch Bowl. It was about a hundred yards from the house.

Steve and I found out fairly early on during our stay that the Irish like to drink. Our first 'closing time' experience happened in the middle of the day when they called 'time' and locked everyone *in*. We thought this was the best thing that had ever happened. Another time we decided to start a health regime and went for a jog en masse. Unfortunately, we only got as far as the Punch Bowl and Steve threw up over the wall on to the street. Alas, that was the end of our workout and we went in for a pint.

I continued jogging but also continued drinking. It wasn't too long before I experienced my first real blackout and it scared the shit out of me. This was different to passing out, as I had done before. This was literally not being able to remember where I had been and what I had done. The incident happened after Steve and I had gone on an afternoon binge. We had been driving drunk, which was and is absolutely unacceptable, and woke up back at the house wearing Rolex and Cartier watches that we'd unknowingly purchased; there was also another earring on me. I had parked Joe's car at a 45-degree angle to the curb, left the car running, gone inside the house and fallen asleep. I didn't remember any of it. That event was my cue that I needed to chill out on this kind of behaviour. It also was the advent of me working out. I would run along the coast road in the morning to try to get in shape. As I began to cut down on the drinking, I gained at least two extra hours in the day in which I would normally be recovering from a hangover. I liked this. However, this wouldn't be my final call for getting on the wagon.

I felt more focused, more in control. And that was a good place to be, since we had a lot of work ahead of us. We wrote all the songs that would become *Hysteria*. Mutt told us the last thing we needed to do was make another album like *Pyromania*, as every other rock band out there in the universe was trying to re-create that sound. Mutt said, 'Look, let's not make *Pyromania II*. Everybody else is trying to do that album now. Let them. We're going to do something different.'

Mutt wanted us to instead create a rock version of Michael Jackson's *Thriller*, our biggest competition on *Pyromania* and the biggest-selling album of all time. *Thriller*'s hit singles crossed over to virtually every audience. Mutt wanted our songs to cross over beyond just rock audiences.

It was a pretty exciting premise. The idea of going beyond *Pyromania* was exactly what we needed to be thinking. *Don't rest on your laurels, try to top yourselves each time out.* Why not use *Thriller* as a sort of model, something to aspire to? Plus, I was a huge fan not just of Michael Jackson but of Prince, soul, funk and Motown as well. I was probably a bit more open to different genres than the other guys in the band.

Steve had got into listening to quirkier, more diverse artists and genres, plus he found inspiration in his love of classical music.

Mutt was adamant that this album would define whether we'd be just a good band with a hit album or a great band with classic, long-standing hits, but we'd have to be totally open-minded and work harder than mere mortals were usually prepared to work. We took chances – in particular on a bigger, brighter, commercial sound that incorporated lots of new technologies. Pop music artists like Michael Jackson, Prince, the Police, Frankie Goes to Hollywood, the Fixx and even INXS could be heard on all kinds of radio stations. All these bands had big, bold, wonderful sounds using the latest technology. The music that was crossing genres was also crossing racial barriers. For the most part, hard-rock bands were kind of stuck in their own box and didn't broaden their own spectrums much. Stay in your genre. Never experiment. Don't be adventurous. We didn't want to be one of those rock bands. We wanted to adapt the brazen attitude of these premier pop acts while keeping the credibility and the distinct sound of a rock band. A tall order, but we had a solution: merge attitudes and styles from a variety of influences. And not be shy about it. A great example is what Aerosmith did with Run-D.M.C., with their killer version of 'Walk This Way'. Everyone in our band was excited over this kind of direction.

But in all that revved-up excitement, Mutt gave us some disappointing news. He had promised to produce an album for the Cars and wasn't able to go into the studio with us. He was becoming the hottest producer in the business, in part thanks to the work he had done with us. But we had the songs written, and we had our marching orders. We just had to choose a new producer to help us execute them. There were only really two other producers comparable to Mutt: Trevor Horn and Quincy Jones. Both were busy. We had a very, very short list of other available producers. Jim Steinman was one of them. We had thought that because of his work with Meat Loaf perhaps this would work out. But it didn't. With Steinman, we thought we were getting a Cadillac, but we felt like we were stuck with a Ford Pinto. He would make suggestions but never seemed able to inspire us or push us harder. I think we were under the impression that the *Bat Out of Hell* producer would add something; however, he was that album's songwriter and Todd Rundgren was actually its producer, so we ground to a halt.

Our management parted ways with Steinman. There was really no one else who could have done this album. We had to wait for Mutt. We had a two-year period in Holland where we worked around the clock with various amazing engineers. Neil Dorfsman, Nigel Green and Dave Thoener were among them. But we still weren't getting anywhere near to this mythical sound that we had in our minds. We basically slogged through a very expensive process at the extremely lovely Wisseloord Studios in Hilversum, Holland, not far outside Amsterdam, conveniently, until Mutt finished the Cars album. Thank God our misfires and waiting paid off in terms of Mutt finally being available for us.

Somewhere in the middle of all this, Rick Allen had his accident.

Steve Clark and I were just about to head out for a big night on the town: the town was Paris, the night was New Year's Eve, and the year was 1984. Let's recap what a good place we were in. Our band had recently come off the amazingly successful *Pyromania* tour and had become the biggest band on the planet, seemingly overnight. Steve and I, nicknamed 'the Terror Twins' for our crazed drinking bouts, were excited and about to celebrate. The evening had started out civilized, but then again, it was early.

The phone rang.

'Rick Allen was in an accident. His arm has been severed.' It was Peter Mensch, one of our managers.

'What do you mean, *severed*?'

'It's gone!'

'What?'

'His left arm came straight off.'

Rick and his girlfriend at the time, Miriam, had been driving on New Year's Eve day on the A57, outside Sheffield.

Rick, who was driving his Corvette Stingray, misjudged a curve and crashed through a stone wall before flipping several times. They'd both been wearing seat belts, but Rick was still thrown from the car. Miriam only had a black eye from the accident, but there was Rick left wandering around in the bitter winter cold, looking for his arm in the snow-covered field. A nurse who lived nearby had been coming up the road and, incredibly, she happened to have a full cooler of ice that she was taking to a New Year's party. A cop also stopped to help. A nurse and a cop, a cooler of ice – unbelievable luck. They settled him down – he was obviously suffering from shock – and helped him locate his arm. Then the nurse put it on the ice as they rushed it and Rick to the hospital with police escort. (Yet another amazing story from this night: the nurse and the cop would end up getting married.) At the hospital, the doctors tried to reattach the arm, but it got infected so then they had to amputate.

Holy fuck. Rick was just twenty-one years old; we'd just come off this wild tour and were getting ready for the new album. Thoughts were spinning in my head. Rick was glad to be alive, but he also lived for drumming – how would he survive this? Physically he would probably be OK, but emotionally, how would a twenty-one-year-old rock star handle it?

Arriving in London a couple of weeks later, we were nervous about seeing Rick, who was still recouping at the

Royal Hallamshire Hospital in Sheffield. We had no idea what we were going to say to our friend who was now facing the end of his drumming career. What else to do but go to a pub to have a few brandies before heading into the hospital? When in doubt, have a drink. When not in doubt, have a drink. That's just how it was back then.

When we had drunk up enough Dutch courage, we went to see him. Rick was sitting in his room, all wrapped up like a mummy.

'Hello, Rick,' we said, in shock at how he looked. Seeing him made it real.

Without even saying hello in return, Rick launched into a spirited pitch. 'OK, guys, listen, I've been working on this thing and I'm going to play drums again. But I'm going to use my left foot to do what my left arm used to do and then I'm going to have all of these little pedals and I'll trigger off all these other sounds and everything's going to be OK when I play . . .'

Steve and I looked at each other thinking, *This poor kid, he must be so medicated that he actually thinks he's cool with all of this and that everything is going to be OK. That he's going to be a drummer again.* It was even sadder than we had imagined. He was hallucinating. He hadn't just lost his arm. He had gone mad. How could he think past the pain, much less about ever drumming again?

'I've been practising on the edge of the bed.'

And there was the proof – a pillow on the floor by the

edge of the bed. Rick Allen never had a real job. He had been playing drums all his life. At fifteen Rick was supposed to have a council-appointed tutor travelling with him while he was in the band. I'm not sure if this happened or not. The reason he had to have a tutor was because he couldn't attend school due to touring. He spent his sixteenth birthday playing drums with Def Leppard (I wasn't in the band yet), as they were the support band for AC/DC. In the dressing room, Bon Scott, AC/DC's singer, sang 'Happy Birthday' to him.

We later found out that Mutt had also been to visit him and that Mutt, being Mutt, had said that Rick could still play drums and that a little thing like a loss of a limb could be overcome with Zen-like willpower, lots of practice and the available technology of the time. I also think this inspired Rick to start practising on the pillow.

As Rick continued recovering, we somehow got back to work. We had Mutt back at the helm, and Nigel Green stayed on as the engineer. I said to Mutt one time after the album had been released, 'Why didn't you just scrap all the stuff we'd done and start from scratch?' He replied, 'You guys were so burnt out and fried that I dared not suggest it.' We basically used some of the prior stuff we'd done as a template, but eventually we ended up replacing it all anyway.

*Hysteria* was recorded in three locations – Paris, Dublin and Hilversum in Holland. During some of this time Steve,

Rick and I all lived together in Donnybrook, Dublin, in this brilliant house that our friends from Spandau Ballet had been renting. I remember us saying to them, 'Wow, this place is really cool!' Gary Kemp, Spandau's guitar player and main songwriter, replied, 'Well, we're leaving to go on tour. Do you want to take on the rent?' And we jumped on it.

This was the house where we would live, and where Rick learned to play drums again. He would set up this electronic drum kit and play from the time he woke up till he fell asleep every single day. We never complained about the noise, as it was one of the most inspiring things I'd ever seen. Rick had to overcome not only the drumming difficulties but everyday things that we take for granted like standing up straight, cutting a loaf of bread or tying shoelaces. It was amazing to see Rick's progress. As frustrating for him as it was, he never gave up. It was 'back to the drawing board' until it became natural. To this day when I see him cut some fruit, I worry he may cut his nose off or something. But the 'Ginsu Knives accident award' actually goes to Rick Savage, who on many an occasion has chopped a piece of finger on a breadboard. Watching Rick play the drums was inspiring, but watching him do everything else could initially be quite agonizing and frustrating. It was just so hard. But we knew he'd figure out a way to get it done. Even though we were now back in Dublin, we had never stopped recording. Nothing affected recording the album, as we always did the drums last anyway.

I can remember a time while we were recording *Hysteria* and we stayed in Loosdrecht, a small village in Holland. We were pretty much holed up in the Waterwolf Hotel during one of their worst winters. However, it was beautiful. With Holland being what it is – reclaimed land with no hills – the lakes, waterways and dykes all over the country were frozen, making the whole place look like a Christmas card. Steve, Malvin Mortimer (Steve's guitar tech, who would later become our tour manager), Mike Rogers (my guitar tech at the time) and I would walk across the frozen water like hippie prophets to get to another bar. We all had these great rooms that looked out over the lake, and in midwinter, we were the only residents left in the hotel. So the whole band left all their doors unlocked so we would swan in and out of each other's rooms. The main meeting place was Malvin's room. Malvin would tempt everyone in with his early morning breakfast fry-ups. His room was the social centre for the band. We were a little family of sorts, focused on making a great album.

As Rick continued to get better, we left it up to him as to what he wanted to do. He wanted to tour, for sure, but Rick thought it best that he take another drummer out on the next tour as a back-up just in case all the electronics crashed. His only request was that we find a guy to play along with him. This was further confirmed when Joe and I went to see Phil Collins perform. (By the way, I've always had a bit of a problem sharing a similar name with Mr Collins. There's always a 'comedian' who thinks he's the first one to crack the Collins/Collen joke. This got more complicated when I attended Phil Collins's show and was on the guest list. When I stated my name, the guy at the door assured me 'he' was inside playing. I told him, 'No. I'm Phil COLLEN. I'm on Phil COLLINS's guest list.' After about ten confusing minutes we were let in. To this day there are still people who believe I am the drummer from Genesis.)

When we met up with Phil after the show with his bass player, Leland Sklar (who, joyfully, I'd get to play with many years later), and Phil asked how Rick was getting on. We told him about Rick's two-drummer request. Phil, who thought that was a great idea, said, 'I've been doing that for years with Chester Thompson in Genesis.' This coming from him meant a hell of a lot to Rick and confirmed that he was on the right track.

When we were taking a little break from the album – Mutt had been working us hard and we all craved a little hiatus – it seemed the perfect time to get Rick's idea off the ground. So in the summer of 1986 we started rehearsals with drummer Jeff Rich, a London boy who had been doing session work for years and had done a stint with Status Quo. Jeff played a regular drum kit while Rick played his electronic kit. It sounded thunderously epic, both of them playing together totally locked in synch. It was the boost of confidence Rick needed. As much progress as Rick was making, in the back of our minds we all knew that the real test would be when the band got back onstage.

We hadn't played live for a bit, so to get ready for an upcoming European festival tour, as well as to test Rick and Jeff out, we booked a series of warm-up shows in the middle of nowhere in southern Ireland. The time arrived for the first of the warm-up shows in Ballybunion, down in the south-west, beyond Limerick. We were all good to go onstage. We were just waiting for Jeff Rich to arrive from England, where he had played the night before with Status Quo. However, his plane was delayed and getting to Ballybunion was proving difficult. When we got the message from Jeff at the airport, we were already late going onstage. Rick would have to play on his own. We delayed the show as much as we could, but the time came for us to perform. Rick was thrown in the deep end and totally rose to the occasion. In fact, when Jeff did arrive halfway through our set, he said to Malvin, 'I think he's good to go. He doesn't need me any more.'

We powered through the warm-up shows – they did the job: we sounded great and everyone was really confident – and made it to Donington. It was obviously wonderful for Rick to have achieved this. But now there was the even bigger test – the Donington Festival, where there were about 70,000 people including press and media everywhere waiting to see if Rick Allen could play a Def Leppard set with one arm. This gig was one of the most memorable shows we ever played. Apart from Rick and all of us being on fire, the audience gave an extremely emotional ovation. People were in tears, which choked us up as well. Rick was twenty-two years old. I was twenty-eight.

After Donington, we did a bunch of other European festivals, and the reaction to Rick was always the same: loud, proud and triumphant. It was always beautiful to watch the audience react to his efforts. Mission accomplished. He was going to be able to carry on. We still needed to finish the *Hysteria* album, so we soon returned to Holland.

While we were back in the Hilversum recording studio, I heard that Mick Jagger was there working on his second solo album, *Primitive Cool*, just down the hall. Supposedly, he also had Jeff Beck on guitar in there along with Simon Phillips on drums. So I was listening at the door one day, my ear pressed up against it, straining to hear anything at all. I was dying to know what was going on inside. All of a sudden the door opened and I practically fell through. And who had opened it but Mick Jagger himself. As I fumbled and tried to explain myself, Jagger invited me in, saying, 'Hey, man. Come in!' He told me to take a seat on the couch so I could listen to what they were working on. There was Jeff Beck in the flesh with his Stratocaster on the other side of the glass.

But on my side of the glass, right in that very room,

Jagger picked up the microphone and started singing the live vocals right in front of my face. It was pretty surreal. I actually showed Mick around our studio and we had some pretty cool chats. When Mick came into our studio once there were a few tabloid newspapers on the table in front of us. Someone picked up a copy and he said, 'You know you shouldn't read that. It'll pollute your mind.' Nowadays we quote this phrase all the time and never has it been more relevant than in this day and age, thanks to gutter/reality TV. There is a very knock-on negative effect on its entranced disciples.

Another band that was in the studio at the same time as us was Mink DeVille. They were great guys from New York City working on their album *Sportin' Life*. One day they asked us to come in and sing on a track called 'Italian Shoes', so we did. Ironically, this was the same room in which I'd previously recorded the guitar solo for 'Animal'.

Mink DeVille also told us later that they loved us being in the studio because every day after we were finished recording they would go and eat all the leftovers that we had left in the studio kitchen. Actually, they were partaking in the over-ordering of food.

Adding to the entirely bizarre experience that the making of *Hysteria* had become – the false starts through Rick Allen's tragic accident and all of the months we burned with other producers and engineers before Mutt came back – was the night that we almost lost Mutt himself.

In November 1986, while we were recording in Holland, our friends in Iron Maiden were playing nearby in Leiden. We knew the guys in the band and got on great with them, so we all wanted to see them play live. We made plans to head over there. Before we left, Mutt warned us not to let Rick Allen stay out too late because there were some drum parts he wanted to complete later in the evening. That didn't happen, as we didn't see Rick for the rest of the night. Meanwhile, this changed plans for Mutt, who left the studio. He had a car accident that night, which resulted in him breaking his leg – though it could have been a lot more serious. This, however, didn't slow us down as much as I thought it would. Mutt bounced back in to the studio with his leg in a cast and a hospital bed complete with controls, from which he continued as if nothing had ever happened. And good thing, since we were putting finishing touches on the rest of the album, which was already two years late.

One day Joe was sitting in the corridor goofing off on a guitar and singing a very simple, almost nursery rhyme-like vocal. A little bit of a phrase, over and over.

Mutt looked at him and said, 'What is that?'

And Joe answered, 'I don't know. Just a little thought I have.'

Within ten days, and at Mutt's insistence, we'd recorded that 'little thought' – a song called 'Pour Some Sugar On

Me'. 'Sugar' had all the elements of rap and country music. Mutt came up with the intro guitar riff and played it with his fingers. It actually sounded very country. When Mutt told me to try it, I was told my finger picking sucked. He told me to play it the way I would play it. So I played it with a metal guitar pick, making a weird hard-rock/country hybrid that you hear on the record today.

Joe's vocal on the verse is reminiscent of a lot of popular rap music at the time, like Public Enemy and Run-D.M.C. I was loosely inspired by the 'verse guitar riff' of Grandmaster Flash's bass line on 'White Lines'. Mutt said that it sounded a bit complex and to put a gap where the snare drum was. That changed the whole feel of it and gave it this very hard-rock-style riff with a rap-style vocal metre over the top. Usually, people don't mix genres within one song. And rock bands hardly liked rap music. But if you listen to another record Mutt produced, AC/DC's *Back in Black*, that title track also contains a rap-style vocal metre. Mutt did a similar thing with us on 'Sugar' and it worked beautifully. The song, in the verses, worked less as a melody and more as a collection of rhythmic sounds, and then all of this was rewarded with a big, sing-along, hooky chorus, 'Pour some sugar on me', that had this amazing melody. In a nutshell, that was the whole hybrid approach Mutt encouraged.

The backing vocals became a defining part of the song. Mutt had me almost screaming the chorus, using a thick, throaty chest voice that actually hurt for days after. When I told him this he said, 'Yeah, but it sounds great!' It was that huge chest-beating machismo that was the perfect antithesis to a grown man requesting to have sugar poured on him.

Mutt liked us to sing that way to differentiate us from all the other bands that sang harmonies, like the Beach Boys and Journey. We maintained an almost punk bravado ethos where we would scream in tune, making us sound different even from our heroes, Queen. This effect and attitude gave the song an extra power. We've always used our backing vocals as another instrument – hence that's why we spent so much time on them – in the studio and live. The last-minute addition proved to be the best decision we ever made. The album was finally completed with the recording of 'Pour Some Sugar On Me' in Holland.

The record company wasn't too thrilled about recording yet another song on an album that had already taken two years, but Mutt was convinced that this could be *the* most important single on the album. It also pushed the album's already long run time to an unprecedented sixty-three minutes of music. Again Mutt said, 'I think this new CD thing is really where it's going to be. When you put too much information on vinyl records, like too many songs, you lose quality. But with everything going toward digital, all of that will change.' So in this case length didn't matter.

While we waited for Mutt and Mike Shipley to mix *Hysteria*, the band members had some downtime. I took this break to officially stop drinking completely. To be exact, it was on 14 April 1987. That was Liz's birthday. We would be on and off again for a few more years to come and were in Paris together when I announced, 'I'm not drinking after your birthday. Really, I'm not.' We had a glass of champagne each and that was it. She stopped as well. We would always support each other on stuff like that. Liz is Jewish, and whenever she fasted on Yom Kippur I would do it with her so she wouldn't have to face the headaches on her own. I had slipped back into social drinking again, and I knew where that would lead, so it really was time to stop. I felt like I gave myself a huge chunk of life back that day.

The next day, we left for India on holiday. I'd always wanted to visit this mystical place. It was different to any place I had ever been. It was LIFE at its most extreme. India was teeming with movement – unlike, say, a city like New York, which seems frenetic at times. In India it felt like the energy was different, along with the colours, aromas and textures.

I remember one of the first impressions I had when I saw people sleeping everywhere in the street at night in Bombay. I thought they were dead bodies at first, so I asked the driver of my car from the airport, 'Shit! What's going on here? Why are all these bodies by the side of the road?'

He replied, 'They're just people sleeping. They live in villages that are too far out so they sleep on the side of the road and just go back to work the next day in the city.'

I've been back to India a few times since. Now it's drastically changed and has become Westernized. There are big modern buildings and skyscrapers everywhere and what seems to be a loss of culture. There were certainly some painful images that remain, like people with no fingers begging at the airport (having had their fingers cut off as small children to make them more appealing to receive money from tourists). But among all the extremes we experienced in India, they were some of the happiest, most enlightened people I have ever met in my entire life. Once Liz and I went back to Paris from India, we were far more relaxed and felt as if our souls had been cleansed a bit. And it was time to hear the final mix of *Hysteria* that Mutt and Mike Shipley had been slaving away on for the last few months.

When Steve and I heard the completed album, we felt we had achieved an artistic apex and that if the only people who bought this album were our parents then that would be more than enough. It was the best thing we'd ever done and it was way beyond any of our expectations or our ambitions. Plus we finally had an album title. It was suggested by Rick Allen after seeing the word *hysteria* on a trashy British tabloid. He said, 'Ay, that would be a good album title, huh?'

Completing the package, I also loved the *Tron*-style art that our graphic designer, Andie Airfix, created. It was a perfect visual backdrop for the way the record sounded – very high-tech and futuristic. *Hysteria* sounded international, iconic and very expensive. It turned out to be all three.

Right before *Hysteria* was released we were all back in Dublin and went to see Elton John, who was in town. Me, Steve and a bunch of Elton's people hung out after the show and went back to his hotel room. For an entire night we sat there spellbound. It was like a master class on the industry. He told us the most amazing, hysterical stories and anecdotes and spoke about his experience in the industry thus far. It was fascinating to hear a real icon talk that frankly about a path we were about to embark on ourselves.

The album dropped 3 August 1987. We were excited to get it out because we thought it was the best thing since sliced bread but were also nervous about how much debt we had incurred recording it. But things were lining up well, and initial reviews were positive, especially MTV's take:

*This album sounds terrific. Every track sparkles and burns. There is no filler . . . A veteran producer of such metal superstars as AC/DC and Foreigner, Lange is a genre master, and this LP is thick with his trademarks: the deep, meaty bass sound; the fat, relentless drums; the dazzling guitar montages; the impeccable sense of structure and separation; the preternatural clarity.*

*Metal Hammer* magazine jumped on board, too, naming *Hysteria* 'Album of the Month' and stating:

*Well, it was something like three years in the making and Def Leppard suffered all sorts of severe trauma during that time, but came out the other side with an album that any major band would be proud to count as one of their catalogue. Not only have Leppard superseded the achievements made with* Pyromania, *but they have come up with a collection that will finally see them broken on a massive scale in Europe, which will be especially sweet for them as they were without acclaim in their own country, the UK.*

To satisfy the ever-growing demands of MTV, we set up a soundstage in Holland and started making videos for the album. This time out, we were more hesitant about doing videos than we had been for *Pyromania*. A lot of things in the industry had changed since the last album, and it seemed like videos were being made en masse and were stale, perfunctory and at times downright silly. It wasn't really about doing anything cool any more, but I suppose that was just the natural progression of things. MTV was so universally huge by now, and things just had to look and feel bigger onscreen. That said, as grandiose as it was, the video for 'Animal' was actually pretty cool. The video's concept was built around a circus theme, and the elaborate production made us feel we essentially joined the circus for two days. In filming one scene, the director told me, 'Hey, when you play the guitar solo we'll have a guy throwing knives around you.' I said, 'Fuck that, there's no way you're throwing a knife at me.' They wound up talking Joe into it, and when you watch the video, you can see him really flinch when the knives strike. Malvin, Steve's guitar tech at the time, even got a part balancing a guitar on his nose.

We filmed the 'Women' video in a dockland area in Amsterdam. And for 'Sugar', we shot in an abandoned hotel that was being demolished in Dublin. In hindsight, I don't think the video represented the song very well. It lacked the sort of style and hipness (for the time) that our other videos always embraced. Fortunately, though, we'd get another shot at a music video for this song, and that time I think we got it right.

'Animal' gave us our first top-ten hit in our home country of England, but the single 'Women' did nothing in the States. We had high hopes for the album itself – we thought it would just explode. And it did, in England. When the album dropped, it went straight to No. 1.

But, in America, *Hysteria* failed to ignite. Our numbers were OK, but it didn't do what *Pyromania* had been doing. We were in the hole for about $4.5 million, which meant we would have to sell at least five million units to break even. We stalled at three million. I know I'm complaining about going 'triple platinum', but this is where we ended up after three and a half years in studio time. In the red. To top it all off, there were some critics who had no problem telling us that we were finished and indulgent, that the album didn't sound rock enough, it sounded too pop, and that it was 'all over for Joe Elliott and the little girls'.

But we carried on. We had already hit the road for the *Hysteria* tour in June, and we played in Europe throughout the summer and into early autumn. From there we would hit the United States, beginning in October and ending in February 1988, and then come back and hit Europe again before heading off to the Far East.

While we were in Europe, Peter Mensch came up with an ingenious idea after seeing a production by Frank Sinatra. Using an 'in the round' presentation, the old crooner was able to roam the stage more freely and connect with fans in a more intimate way. It changed the dynamics of a concert. All of a sudden, there were really no 'bad' seats. So we would play 'in the round' – meaning the stage would be where a boxing ring would be: stationary, in the middle of the arena, which basically meant four front rows for the audience, giving everyone in the hall an equal view of the band when we came to America. It made for a spectacular show once we got the feel for it – and it totally affected how we were as performers. Everyone does it nowadays, but back then it was a novel thing for a rock band to do. Phay MacMahon, who was our lighting designer at the time (and who is our production manager today), came up with the actual set designs. He had some brilliant ideas about how to bring it all together.

PHAY MACMAHON: It may not seem like it today, but back in 1987 the Def Leppard stage set-up for *Hysteria* was really something out of this world. Their manager, Peter Mensch, had the idea to do a show in the round. The only band up to that point that had really attempted something like that was Yes, back in the late 1970s.

Performing in the round was good for a number of reasons. The first was, obviously, the entire arena would get equally great looks at the band, because the guys would be free and mobile to run all over the place. The other thing was the fact that you could place it in the middle of an arena meant that you could also sell many more seats that would otherwise be lost behind the stage.

As for the design of the stage itself, it truly was state-of-the-art. The album artwork was plastered on the floor of the thing, and it had several different levels and a rotating drum set for Rick. It also had a very uncluttered look and feel to it, because all of the guitar techs worked underneath the stage, and all of the guitar amps were also located offstage.

The lighting rig was also wonderful and elaborate and featured many movable parts and lasers that had never been used for concerts before. We would hang four black curtains featuring the album artwork around the stage before they came out for their first song.

There was some short intro music, and then, as the

band kicked into 'Stagefright' the curtains would drop to reveal the boys.

Now, the only thing was, how do you get the band to the stage? The stage itself had no facilities for changing rooms or anything. It was just a stage; but it did have some space underneath it where the guys could be brought up from. So here's what we did.

After the opening band, Queensrÿche, finished up, we would drop the curtains to hide the stage. Then we had these big things that look like laundry baskets to help cart off Queensrÿche's gear. What we would do shortly before it was time for Def Leppard to take the stage was to put the guys in these baskets, cover them up and then secretly wheel them to the stage. They would literally be within touching distance of thousands of fans as we wheeled them out, but nobody was the wiser. They thought we were just moving gear back and forth!

So we'd wheel them out before the show, get them settled underneath the stage, and from there they would just wait until their cue to come out and play. Then of course, after the show was done, they had to wait there until the arena emptied out, because there was nowhere for them to go.

If we did it today, I'm sure there would be some elaborate tunnel or passage that would allow them to move back and forth as they wanted before the show. But in the late 1980s it was a much more primitive system, even though it looked very high-tech. But, for the most part, we never had too many issues or technical screw-ups. I do remember one night at the Nassau Coliseum, before the band came out, when the air-conditioning system under the stage got hold of one of the huge drapes we used and sucked it in. So we recruited the audience to get the curtain pulled out from the AC system, and they actually were very helpful, yanking it loose like [in] a huge tug-of-war.

As ingenious as the whole thing was, there were also many booby traps on that thing, with all of the lasers and trapdoors and ramps and things. And slopes that were sometimes dangerous for the boys. I think everyone slid off that stage at least once. But not like Steve. He actually fell off one night just before the lasers came on, and then we couldn't find him. He had disappeared in the crowd and we had to fish him out. Joe and Phil may have been the only two to not have serious accidents on that stage. But it was still all pretty wonderful and very memorable.

We had seen a small-scale version of the stage while touring Europe, but nothing could prepare us for seeing the real thing the first time, in Glens Falls, New York. For all of us, it felt like entering a giant spaceship. It looked like that and it felt like that. The five of us wandered inside and outside of it, exploring it like excited kids in a cave. It was massive. Huge challenges came with such an untested concept, and

I'm sure other bands might have said, 'Forget it, this is never going to work.' As 'high-tech' as it was at the time, though, it was actually sort of primitive when you got right down to it. But we worked out the glitches and made it happen. That's how we handled everything.

We kicked off the US tour and premiered our spectacular new stage in Glens Falls on 1 October 1987. There were problems: given the size and strange design of it, it took the crew all night to load out. The next night, for our show in Albany, it took the crew a ridiculous amount of time to load in, which made us think we might have bitten off more than we could chew. But the crew got the hang of it all and in the end it proved to be the most remarkable and innovative design that had ever been taken on the road. And, most important, fans would love it because there was no bad seat in the house.

We all had up to six different microphones placed in various locations on the stage. We always had that team-effort attitude, supporting Joe as front man and working together to put on a unified performance. On this new stage, we were all free to run around and live out our wildest rock star fantasies if we wanted to. But that's not how we were – we were like a football team. You know when you watch a really good team, like Barcelona? It's about how they cover the field, about great passing and creating space. That was our strategy on the stage. We worked as a team to provide full coverage of the field or, in this case, our massive and beautiful new stage in the round. And it was a workout: I can remember coming offstage after performing a three-hour set and feeling like I was eighty years old – and I was only thirty.

The fans loved the spectacle. The only hiccup was, with the album not exactly burning up the charts (nor the singles), we were not getting huge crowds. It felt a bit silly mounting that huge stage to a half-full arena. And it seemed that even MTV couldn't save us.

With all the amazing concert performances and an incredible album, we couldn't understand why we still failed to ignite. We toured through the end of 1987 and into early 1988: it was gruelling night after night, but still the crowds were not what we had hoped. After the release of our third single, 'Hysteria', in March, we returned to Europe to tour. To our surprise, it was our most successful European tour to date. It was a real reversal to have such a great reception in Europe, where people once bemoaned our American success, compared to the tepid reception in America, where folks had adored us.

It was on this European leg of the *Hysteria* tour that I got to know Scott Smith, the bass player from the band Loverboy, when they opened for us. We hit it off almost instantly and became really good friends. He was a bit older than me, and his band had been around longer, so he would always give me advice on things like management, money and other parts of the business. You don't get many lasting relationships out on the road, but Scott and I would remain close through the years.

We would be out on tour for over a year promoting the album. Remember, there was no such thing as social media, so there were a lot of personal appearances and interviews on top of performing practically every night. This was the first tour that I had not touched a drink. It felt really weird; the best way I can describe it is that it felt a little out of context to still be jumping around in a rock band. I'd always associated, as everyone else had, the drinking with the whole rock star thing. I was the only guy in the group who was completely sober. There were people who would say, 'Just have one drink,' and I would have to tell them, 'No. If I start, I can't stop.' A glass of wine would turn into a bottle of wine, and that would be a bottle of Jack Daniel's by the end of the week. But I didn't fall off the wagon once. It was never tempting, because when I made that decision I stuck to it. But while I avoided alcohol, I watched Steve's drinking get worse by the day. We started talking about the alcohol as a problem, which Steve definitely acknowledged. But it's easier said than done to just stop.

While we continued to tour Europe, a funny thing was happening back in America. 'Sugar' was suddenly blowing up the airwaves across the country. Apparently, radio stations in Florida started getting lots of requests from strippers who were dancing in a frenzy around poles to

'Sugar', their newest stripper anthem. The song was starting to catch on like wildfire and spread to the point that it catapulted the *Hysteria* album to number one on the *Billboard* charts. Amazing. Up until then, the album had sold about three million copies, not even enough to cover the cost of making it. So we took advantage of it. We cut a new video using concert footage from our Denver show; it was big, bold and stylish, like it should have been the first time we did it. That concert video shot to the top of MTV's *Dial MTV* show and sat there for eighty-five straight days, tying with the longest run ever. The song went to No. 1 in Canada, No. 2 in America, and No. 18 on the British singles chart. Most importantly, it reinvigorated the album. After a tour of Asia in May, we returned to the States to tour from the rest of May into August.

Our triumphant return was humbling: we had been here before, so we appreciated all the new attention we were getting, but we also realized how fickle human nature can be, so while everyone was blowing smoke up our asses, we took mental note to stay cool. But we did cheer when Tony DiCioccio, our former tour accountant from Q Prime Management, told us the US promoters were seriously interested in doing another multi-night, multi-city US tour to carry on through September. They felt it would be hugely successful with our newfound base. We said OK. We were in. I mean, who could say no to that?

*

As it turned out, they were right. The tour was huge. Fucking monstrous. Everywhere. We played the Rupp Arena in Lexington, Kentucky. Back in 1987 we had a very vibrant 3,000 people show up, but a dismal empty 20,000 seats. In 1988, the very same venue was sold out. It was back to pop star status. The same would be true at the Tacoma Dome in Washington State. We went from 11,000 people in 1987 to 30,000 sold-out seats in 1988. Once near-empty arenas across the country were now selling out in a matter of minutes.

We had thought that because of how the record sounded, and not just because of how much work we put into it, it would explode. The first single, 'Animal', gave us our first top-ten hit in England. *Hysteria* the album went straight to number one. We thought the album would have the same effect in America. It didn't. *Hysteria* failed to ignite. We were doing OK numbers in America, but it didn't do what *Pyromania* had been doing.

Once again, we learned to take everything with a pinch of salt. At the beginning of the *Hysteria* tour cycle, people's attitudes toward us as a band and toward the album were very cynical and disrespectful. We were well aware that we were not being doted on for the lyrical content of our music. We always felt it important to create escapism through our music. That's why you don't see our lyrics being married at all to political messages and whatnot. The music we make is *Star Wars* for the ears and sonically pleasing. Now that this thing was going through the roof, it was clear that some of the same people's current attitude, which appeared to be supportive, felt extremely fake to us. You can always rely on humans to be typical and disappointing. The band appreciated the album for what it was and all the hard work we had put in. It absolutely reminded us how shallow the entertainment industry is. But, if they liked you – even if it was only for the time being – they liked you.

We were playing in Chicago and Robert Plant showed up backstage to pay us a visit. Everybody in Def Leppard is a huge Led Zeppelin fan. I kept thinking back to when I saw Zeppelin as a kid back in the mid-1970s and couldn't believe that Robert Plant actually wanted to come see our show. But it got better. When he heard about the way we got wheeled out there every night, he got all excited and asked if he could be a part of the clandestine operation that took place before the show. It's amazing how primitive the whole 'getting to the stage' thing was. But that is theatre for you. Smoke and mirrors has always been a major part of its entertainment. Plant asked if he could actually be one of the guys that wheeled the laundry hampers to the stage. Cool. Robert Plant, one of the most recognizable rock-and-roll icons on earth, put on a disguise, with a bandana around his head, some dark shades and a leather jacket. I remember he looked a bit like a pirate. Me and Sav said, 'Fuck! Robert Plant's pushing us out!' as we were crouched in the bottom of the hamper. Sav and I would share a cart, as would Joe and Steve. Rick would've already gone to the stage, because he would go sometimes to warm up playing under the stage along with whatever band was opening up for us. Then he would wait for us to join him. Rick would wear a disguise, along with a fake arm holding a beer. At one of the gigs he had on a baseball cap, a jacket, glasses and this arm. Steve went up to him, patted him on the back and said to him, 'Have a good show, Rick!' while sticking a sign on his back that read *I Am Rick Allen*. No one noticed. We played extra hard that night, knowing that Robert Plant was watching us, and it wouldn't be the last time he came to one of our shows. (Years later, in 1993, he would again join us onstage at a gig, in Copenhagen, to play a medley of some Zeppelin classics.)

Just after the New Year, in January 1989, 'Rocket' became the seventh single from *Hysteria* to be released in the States. And it made it into the top fifteen on the *Billboard* charts. It was a nice cap to a hard-won album release. It had been a slog – the recording of it, touring it and promoting it. But we'd sweated blood over it and had spent close to $5 million to get it done, so it would need to be successful. We thought it was the best thing we had ever done and the best thing we had ever heard. It was a combination of all the rock influences we had ever heard, culminating into a palatable, accessible monster. We kept going until it was a success. We knew it would be. We just had to convince everyone else. And we did: *Hysteria* would go on to dominate many album charts around the world for three years. It wound up spending ninety-six weeks in the US Top 40 and to date has sold more than twenty million copies.

In a sense, the end of the *Hysteria* tour signalled the end of an era for Def Leppard. We didn't know it yet, but *Hysteria* was the last album the band ever did where all five guys were single. It was that last stage of an era when we were all free of any real responsibilities beyond just being together and making music. After that, for whatever reason, everything changed. When you're in your early twenties, *if* you're driven and have a goal in mind, *everything* becomes secondary – relationships, family, everything, even if you don't like to admit it. Once you achieve that goal, you take your foot off the gas and it's very hard to get back to that place, especially now that you're in your thirties. Your focus changes, because you've achieved the objective, and what you did naturally becomes contrived. Now you have the focus of a thirty-year-old man, and although you have experience, you don't have that twenty-year-old reckless, driven abandon that got you to this point. This happens to a lot of people in the entertainment industry. As you get older, you start thinking about other things. In a nutshell, in our youth we're selfish and not aware of anything else. As we get older, our narcissism gets diluted (at least it's supposed to), almost as if we're moving to a higher astral plane. So at the end of the *Hysteria* tour, our lives began to open up.

We had still been on tour when I first met Jacqueline Long. I met her at Great Woods amphitheatre in Mansfield, Massachusetts, just outside Boston. Jacki was a model and lived in New York City but had been at a show with two of her girlfriends. I thought she was lovely and got her phone number. In typical Phil Collen fashion, I failed to mention all of this to my girlfriend Liz. Needless to say, the shit hit the fan when Liz found out. We broke up, and Jacki and I started seeing each other.

When we finally finished the tour, I was straddling between London and New York, and I still had my place in Paris; I felt a little confused about where I actually lived. But since I was spending a lot more time with Jacki, I decided to move in with her. Her tiny apartment in Manhattan's SoHo neighbourhood couldn't fit any of my shit – guitars and stuff. So we went house-hunting and found a badass loft near the corner of West Broadway and Houston. This place was amazing, not to mention Sting lived in the loft directly above me. The ceilings were really high and the large windows ran the length of the loft's redbrick walls. It was perfect, the quintessential industrial SoHo loft, and a real sanctuary in the middle of a chaotic city.

Just as we were moving in, we found out Jacki was pregnant. We had already decided to get married, but this sped things up just a bit. Jacki and I were married in the summer of 1989. Our son, Rory James Collen, was born on 4 January 1990. Up until that point in life, I had never even held a child. I had been in London prior to that, writing some songs, but Jacki said the doctor informed her that I should probably 'come home now'. So I jumped on the Concorde and flew from London to New York post-haste only to sit for another two weeks waiting for Rory to make an appearance.

Coming off the *Hysteria* world tour, we knew we did not want to take another four years to release our next album. So we barely took a break and soon met up in Amsterdam with Mike Shipley – who had mixed *Hysteria*, done many a Def Leppard session and worked with Mutt on many projects as producer and engineer – along with Pete Woodroffe, his assistant. We started recording the demos that we had been writing with Mutt. Mike would send Mutt the recordings as we got them done.

As always, Amsterdam was a fascinating place. I had at least three different apartments over the course of my stay there, all in or around the red-light district, so I saw it all. It is a maze of old, narrow streets that boast endless store-fronts with girls selling their 'wares'. Most are seated in various stages of undress. Men and women travel from all over the world just to stand in front of the windows and stare. It's as much a tourist attraction as it is a sex mecca. Amsterdam is also famous for its coffee shops that offer up cannabis, sinsemilla and other THC-containing products, all legal in Holland. I would walk every morning and every night through the streets just to take it all in.

Looking back, it was probably not the best environment for Steve. As we got down to work writing the album, it became clear to all of us that that he was worse than ever. There was more responsibility as we got older and more successful, and we were all starting families. My sobriety was still incredibly important to me, and I would not jeopardize it. But for Steve it all just kept getting worse.

Things had changed for me when I met Jacki. I used to hang with Steve all the time. But once I began spending my time with her, I lost track of what he was doing and who he was doing it with. It wasn't that I considered myself his keeper, but he was certainly my closest friend and I loved him. When I was around him, there was less chance of him spinning off the rails, especially with me being stone cold sober. There are functioning alcoholics, which I think Steve had been for a long time. But he was now entering a phase that seemed much more dark and dangerous. He was no longer himself.

In a way, Steve didn't have that much choice in the matter. He was surrounded by drink most of his life. Steve's dad was a taxi driver and I think Steve was always trying to prove that he was worthy of his rock star status. In England, and I'm sure everywhere else in the world, excessive drinking often gets covered up, even with serious alcoholics. The attitude is often, 'Oh, he just likes a drink,' brushing aside the problem. It is hard to come away from that environment unscathed. In addition, it wasn't enough that he had become an extremely successful musician in one of the most famous bands on the planet. There was still this thing about the culture he came from. Steve had to prove his manhood all of the time, that he had the values of a Sheffield steelworker underneath his golden splendour.

One morning Steve called me at about eight and asked if he could come over to my apartment. 'I've got something to show you,' he said.

I found it odd that he was up so early (I was the one who was usually up early) so I told him to come on over. What was going on? Our little studio apartments were basically next to each other, so it took him just a minute to be at my door. When he showed up, he held his hand out straight. I noticed that it was shaking almost uncontrollably. He said he was like this every day now and that he would go to a bar to get a drink and make the shaking stop. 'That is the only way I can see you guys and look kind of normal,' he admitted. I suddenly realized how serious this was. But I was also relieved, in a sense, because for the very first time he was addressing the fact that something was wrong. I didn't want to get my hopes up too high, but it was a positive step, this acknowledgement.

Soon after that, I had a terrible dream that Cliff Burnstein called me to say Steve had died. It woke me up in the middle of the night, and as I lay there thinking about it, it didn't seem like that far a stretch. Steve called me a few weeks later from a hospital in Paris. He'd gone on a bender and had got alcohol poisoning. I flew in from London, where I had been during a break in recording, and when I arrived, there he was, hooked up to an IV, head down. He didn't want to look at me. He was embarrassed and ashamed, especially after recently admitting that he had a problem. I said, 'Steve, I'm here for you. We all are. But first you've got to realize you've got a problem.' We still didn't really know much about alcoholism, but that seemed pretty basic. Address that you have a problem.

All of us knew that Steve had a problem, but none of us knew what to do about it; it was a learning curve for all of us. We thought that if you drank too much, you should probably stop. I was able to do it, but it wasn't like that for Steve. We all stopped encouraging any kind of drinking around Steve. Joe and I even accompanied Steve to a few AA meetings in various cities on separate occasions, but Steve really needed to go to an intensive rehab programme. And he wasn't going to get there by himself. Everyone in and around the band's inner circle knew we had to do something – soon.

# 4

In the winter of 1989, a few of us were in the studio one day when we got a call from Mensch. 'Steve's in trouble. He was found unconscious in a bar in Minneapolis, and he's been rushed to a hospital there.'

We flew out to see him immediately. It was me, Joe, Mutt and Tony DiCioccio, and either Peter or Cliff. I remember turning up at the Hazelden Addiction Treatment Center, north-east of Minneapolis. The patients looked like the cast from the film *One Flew Over the Cuckoo's Nest*, including the large Native American. We were each asked by the doctor to write a letter to Steve voicing our opinions and how we felt about all of this. But then the doctor said, 'OK. Now I need you to read it to him.' The doctor also told us about enabling and that if we loved our friend we would have to confront him via intervention. I read my letter first. We all sat in a circle and we told him, 'Steve, you're scaring the shit out of us.' He sat there with a cigarette taking it all in. Mutt gave him a big hug; then we all hugged him and told him that we loved him. That was a very tearful and emotional experience for all involved, especially when the doctor explained to us that about 70 per cent of alcoholics who get to this level usually end up getting killed either by accident or overuse. This was just about as serious as it could get. This was something very different.

The doctor also told us that the alcohol level in Steve's blood was 0.59. That didn't really mean anything to us, until he explained that it was a 0.41 level that had killed John Bonham from Led Zeppelin. Then he went into detail about just how dire it was – more statistics about alcoholism, the physiological and psychological toll on the body, everything. Then family members and friends of alcoholics at the facility came in with their stories.

With our support, Steve went to another rehabilitation centre, this time in Tucson, Arizona. We told him to take a six-month sick leave and get healthy – that we'd keep working on the record and that, as soon as he was able to, he'd get back in the fold. It wasn't long afterward that Steve met Janie Dean, another patient who was being treated for heroin addiction. Steve thought this would be great – they could help each other cope with each other's addictions. But, as anyone familiar with addiction knows, this was a bad fucking idea. They both left rehab and continued aiding each other's addictions. We didn't think it could get worse, but it did. It became almost impossible to keep track of Steve's whereabouts or what he was doing.

The morning of 8 January 1991, I got a call from Cliff.

'Phil,' he said, 'I've got some bad news. Steve died in his sleep.' It was exactly like the dream I had had. What had happened was that he had been drinking and had cracked a rib earlier on. The doctor told him not to drink while taking his pain medications. He drank anyway. The coroner's report, I believe, read that it was due to a swelling of the brain. Janie had found him at his Chelsea house in London. The very surreal part about it for me was that I had expected a phone call like this perhaps from Cliff for the past five years, so I wasn't shocked but instead freaked out. This was such a huge psychological blow for all of us. After Rick's accident and amazing recovery, we hadn't thought we'd ever have to confront anything like this but now one of us had died. It's incredible that we never prepare for death while we're young, almost as if we have this immortal streak in us. Janie was not to be of this world for much longer either. We heard a few years later that she also died from drug use.

Initially, I didn't even want to be in the band after Steve passed. It just didn't seem right to replace him. Steve Clark had been such an integral part of the band; he had been instrumental in creating the sound and was part of this family that we had. I mean, you wouldn't replace a brother if he died. It's funny – many people have said to me over the years, 'It's great you kept Rick after his accident,' as if it's only about being in a commercialized music group. I have to say, I always feel quite insulted by that statement. We're a lot deeper than that. We *chose* to be together in this band, and we've spent more time together than most blood-related families. If you consider it, kids usually leave their parents' households in their twenties if they're lucky. But we have thirty-something years together under our belt.

With all this being said, one morning Joe and I were in the kitchen and I said, 'I'm done. I don't want to do this any more.' One of us had gone and the gang was broken. He said, 'Well, what do you want to do?' I told him I'd rather be a plumber. (A bit ridiculous, considering I can barely turn a faucet off. But you get the idea.)

But Joe talked me off the ledge, saying, 'Don't become a plumber. We owe Steve for all these songs we wrote together on this record. He's still part of us. Let's, at the very least, honour him and finish what we started.'

So I did what Joe suggested: I threw myself into work. For weeks after Steve's death I would go to the studio and play guitar and listen to the parts that Steve had done on our demos – I had to learn his parts and then play them verbatim along with my own. It was just me and Steve in that room. It felt as if there was a ghost in there with me as I played his parts over and over. It was almost as if he was still alive. It was just so weird. But I knew how to put his spin on all those notes. I lost myself in trying to sit there and play along with Steve, working as hard as I could to create something he would have been proud of.

I never really gave in to the emotion, though all that time I was dealing with Steve's death. I had put up many walls so I wouldn't have to deal with it or accept it. It wasn't until about three months later, when I was stuck in traffic on the 101 freeway in Los Angeles and the Rolling Stones' 'Waiting on a Friend' came on the radio that I burst into tears. I pulled over to the side of the road and cried like a baby. I couldn't stop. That was really the moment that I began to deal with the loss of my best friend. To this day, I continue to have dreams where Steve appears and we just talk as if nothing has changed. It feels totally natural, and that's fine with me.

This was the first time anyone in the band had suffered the loss of someone that we saw every day. Although we were all trying to process this, there was something that really started annoying me. It was the fact that when Steve's funeral was announced, all of a sudden, everyone started caring about Steve – from total strangers to people who knew him on the fringe. I was so pissed about this that I decided not to go to the funeral. When Steve needed help, only the people really close to him were there. As soon as he died, everyone jumped in with their 'I knew Steve' stories, not trying to help with his addiction but simply based on trying to hang out with a rock star. The floodgates opened and all the sycophants started pouring in for the funeral, which confirmed my decision not to go. I know Steve would have been with me on that.

The album *Adrenalize* was released in March 1992.

Just to give you a historical timeline, there was social upheaval in America at the time and everything had changed drastically. This is when the LA riots were going off, following the acquittal of police officers in the videotaped beating the year before of black motorist Rodney King. *Adrenalize* hadn't taken us as long as *Hysteria*, but obviously the death of Steve prevented us from completing it as quickly as we had originally planned. And that was fine. As a band, we were now used to dealing with major personal adversities and, in the end, the records would just come out when they came out. But, similarly to when *Hysteria* had been released, the musical landscape had again shifted dramatically. This time, however, it wasn't pretty arena bands like Bon Jovi that had come to rule the world. Now it was the ragged and flannel world of grunge that was taking over, and this was going to be a much tougher environment for us to exist in. In the eighties, it was fairly easy for us to go head-to-head with other powerful arena bands. But bands like Nirvana and Pearl Jam were going to be a whole other story.

I love those bands, actually, and it kind of reminded me of the musical shift when punk first exploded in England. You had the two leaders of the charge, the Sex Pistols and

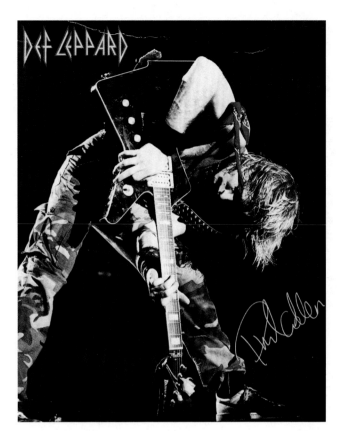

All photos courtesy of Phil Collen. Personal photos unless otherwise indicated.

Jack Murphy Stadium, San Diego, 1983. I love this shot. It's one of my favorite Ross Halfin shots with my Ibanez Destroyer. (Ross Halfin)

Left to right: me, the top of Malvin's head, Mensch, Steve, and Joe. Bangkok, Thailand, 1984.

Liz. (Denis O'Regan)

Me and Steve. Happy Hour somewhere in the world, 1983.

Me with Scott Smith on my birthday.

Rory, Woofie, and my mum. Christmas in Laguna Hills, 1990.

Me and Rory.
(Ross Halfin)

Rory in Trafalgar Square, London.

Me and Rory on a Def Lep private plane during the Adrenalize tour in 1993.

Me and Anita.

**Three generations of Collens: me, Rory, and my dad. San Clemente, CA.**

**My dad's last home. His caravan.**

Me, Viv, and Rick Allen in a village in Ecuador.

Cybernauts Japanese tour. Left to right: Dick Decent, Trevor Bolder, and Woody Woodmansey.

Vivian, Sav, and me in a Guatemalan jungle, hanging with children outside a bullring just before going onstage.

Hang gliding to Copacabana Beach. Rio de Janeiro, Brazil.

Me bungee jumping off the Kawaru Bridge. South Island, New Zealand.

Helen and me having some fun at Laguna Beach. (Mike Steele Photography)

Jumping the broom with Helen in Brooklyn, NY, August 12, 2010.
(Kerika Fields Photos)

Dumb Blonds reunion, London, 2011. Left to right: Pete Webb, me, Freddie Ball, and Jeff Hepting. (Helen L. Collen)

Me and Helen's grand-mother, Hattie Simmons, July 16, 2010, on my and Helen's wedding day in West Palm Beach, Florida. Ms. Hattie passed away March 4, 2015. (Helen L. Collen)

After a workout on tour. Fifty-four years old, 2012. (Helen L. Collen)

Manraze. Shepherd's Bush, London, 2011. (Helen L. Collen)

Getting in a light workout with UFC Light Heavyweight World Champion Jon Jones in Albuquerque, New Mexico. (Helen L. Collen)

Me with Rory all grown up and Shaq (left) and Jackson (far right). (Helen L. Collen)

Me with C. J. Vanston in his studio. (Helen L. Collen)

Me and Helen at
an event in New
York City. (Kerika
Fields Photos)

A test shot in my garage. (Helen L. Collen)

Getting pumped for the stage. Canada, 2015. (Ross Halfin)

My daughter Savannah.

I present the wonderful Charlotte Gerson with an auctioned guitar.

the Clash, and everything else after that was just sort of trying to be like them. In the early 1990s, Nirvana became the wind of change in America. It was the closest thing that America had to Britain's punk explosion. It was different. It changed music, but it was still not as bold and brash as the Pistols and the Clash. Initially, Nirvana was about Kurt Cobain's narrative about his personal demons, which white America could relate to; hence he influenced a whole generation. The music was so ferocious and cool, as was the antifashion – and it worked. A lot of kids could relate to what Kurt was singing about. Pearl Jam's 'Jeremy' was about a kid bringing a gun to school and shooting himself in front of his class. We didn't have that in England. We quickly realized we couldn't compete musically with social commentary that everyone could relate to. Liking a certain kind of music is almost like belonging to a club. People wear the uniform of the club. In this case it was lumberjack shirts and old cardigans. When you are dealing with a social commentary – i.e. punk, rap, hip-hop or grunge – you can't really compete by just being part of a 'musical genre'. We were a rock band, and for the first time in our career that wasn't enough.

It was into this environment that we released *Adrenalize*, which, with all the writing and recording that went into it, immediately seemed outdated. However, that still didn't stop the album from being No. 1 on the *Billboard* charts for six weeks and going quadruple platinum. Had we released that album three years earlier, perhaps it would have been even more relevant. But here in the nineties it was totally irrelevant because of the political and musical landscape. The country's mood was changing. Just like back in the 1960s, race relations and race riots were dominating the headlines, and all of a sudden it seemed like all the progress that had been made over the years had dissolved in a wash of anger, injustice and violence. The world had become far more serious since we first exploded on the scene, and we didn't seem to fit in. Ironically, even though we were on the wane, this is the first and only time we would nab the cover of *Rolling Stone* (and it would just be, sadly, four, not five, of us). The irony is that *Rolling Stone* mag was so trendy at the time, and we were about as hip as haemorrhoids. Still, we ended up on the cover without Steve. The headline on the magazine was 'To Hell and Back' and the focus, of course, was all we had endured in terms of tragedy. It began: 'They say they're not jinxed, but the members of Def Leppard have had to endure a string of tragedies that would have destroyed most bands.'

The record was done, and we had a tour to start. How can you replace a family member? You don't. But you move on.

So instead of auditioning guitar players, we invited five different people down to hang out and play. It wasn't a cattle call, which would have been crap. John Sykes had helped out with some backing vocals on the album. He has the most amazing voice and plays his ass off on guitar. We also contemplated Adrian Smith from Iron Maiden, who I've known for years from him growing up in the same part of London as me; Nick Lashley, who played with Alanis Morissette; Huey Lucas, who was a really good guitar player and wrote really good songs; and Vivian Campbell, who played in Dio and Whitesnake. The main thing was that we had to get along well with whoever we chose, they had to be British – Vivian is from Belfast – and had to know how to sing.

Most people associate Vivian with metal and shredding guitar playing after he played the wonderful solo on Dio's 'Rainbow in the Dark', but that couldn't have been further from the truth. Vivian had been honing his writing skills and practising his singing (technically, Vivian is the best singer in our band). He was more into bands like Crowded House and the Beatles than anything hard rock or metal. Because we could never replace Steve, it was cool that Vivian could bring a different dimension to the band with his voice. Viv had taken singing lessons from Roger Love, a renowned vocal coach. This whole element took our band to another level, as Roger would give us all vocal warm-ups and exercises. This in turn enabled us never to miss another gig due to losing our voices. The vocal blend that Vivian, Rick Savage and I have developed along with Joe freaks me out to this day. When we're onstage, it seems like I'm listening to the record. I remember the first time this happened at a BBC radio session, hearing back the backing vocals that three of us had just done, thinking they sounded so good that they must be a sample. This is something that we pride ourselves on: being one of the very few bands that actually sing their vocals live. This dimension was brought in when Vivian joined the band. Ironically, when Vivian had seen us back in the eighties, he thought we were using samples on our backing vocals. We proved him wrong, but we did work our asses off on getting our vocals to where they are today. Out of the guys we were hanging with playing guitar, Vivian seemed to slot right in with the band. It seemed like a natural progression from being with Steve to being a four-piece for a year to integrating Vivian into the band. Rick Allen can sing, too, but after he bailed on some of the harmonies, we let him off the hook to just play drums.

The first show we played with Viv was at a tiny club in Dublin called McGonagle's. This was to be a warm-up to Vivian's grand entrance at the Freddie Mercury Tribute Concert for AIDS Awareness.

We were all obviously huge Freddie Mercury fans and were very saddened by his death. The interest that Queen guitarist Brian May had taken in Def Leppard always meant a lot to us, and so it was an honour to be invited to play at this show, which was to be held at London's Wembley Stadium for a crowd of about 72,000 people. It was also to be broadcast live on TV and radio stations to more than seventy countries around the world, with an anticipated audience of over one billion people. It really got no bigger than this.

All of the proceeds from the show were going to be used to create the Mercury Phoenix Trust AIDS charity organization. Freddie had died in November 1991 from the disease and, soon after that, his remaining band members had wanted to get together a big show like this to raise money for research. And did they ever make good on that plan. That concert was a who's who of some of our favourite artists. Among those appearing that day were Elton John, Guns N' Roses, David Bowie and Metallica, and the list goes on and on. There was also a full-on geeked-out fan moment for Joe and me when Brian May invited us onstage to sing backing vocals for 'All the Young Dudes' with David Bowie, the remaining members of Queen, Ian Hunter, and Mick Ronson – another one of my heroes. This was actually to be Mick's last performance before he died from cancer.

It was time to rehearse for the *Adrenalize* tour, which would wind up being our longest tour to date – a full year and a half. The venue where we chose to rehearse, for some reason, was the Mediterranean isle of Ibiza, the unofficial centre of European hedonism. This wasn't the first time I'd been to the spectacular Spanish island. Back when I had been in Girl, we'd played in the centre of the old town, a seven-hundred-year-old fort, just spectacular, and as payment we were given a villa to stay in for the week, during which time we were completely out of control. One of my vague memories is of hanging out with the guys from Spandau Ballet and strolling into a restaurant, drunk and completely naked. A waiter tried to cover me up with a napkin. That pretty much sums up my week in Ibiza with Girl. Things were slightly different with Def Leppard. We were focused completely on getting the new version of Def Leppard up and running. The new version of me was a complete teetotaller. We focused very hard on all of the harmonies and just overall basic sounds that we would be needing for the next year and a half.

We were going to be there for the best part of a month, and we took over this hotel called Hotel Victoria, the perfect base for us. It was out of the way, and if you didn't get involved in the insane nightlife of Ibiza, you were left with regular hours of a picture-perfect Mediterranean city. I even flew my mum down to hang out while we were there, and she loved and appreciated it, as she did whenever she visited us during rehearsals in exotic places. It was so funny whenever I'd bring my mum out while I travelled. Its effect created a polar opposite reaction between male and females. The males all said, 'What's wrong with you? Why bring your mum out on the road?' The females would be taking their clothes off for me, thinking it was the most wonderful, thoughtful and surprisingly sexy thing in the world. I always told people, I love my mum and so why wouldn't I have her come and visit? And that was the truth. When Steve and I went to Australia in 1988 for a *Hysteria* promo tour, I brought my mum along – it was just the three of us. I was barely off the flight from London and I was shagging one of the stewardesses, who was simply charmed by the loving act of a son. It always amazed me the effect it had on women.

Looking back, I think we totally over-rehearsed in Ibiza, because my playing was really stiff, and I didn't enjoy it as much. This had an effect on me when it came to our next tour, for the album *Slang*. I would actually stop practising scales and everything I had done pre-*Adrenalize* tour. When I just loosened up and closed my eyes, the playing didn't sound so uptight. As important as the technical side of things is, 'feeling it' is far more important. The club tour went great, all sold out. It was amazing. We used it as a part of the rehearsal process before arenas, and it was fucking expensive! We were operating on an eighties-style hedonistic budget. Looking back, it was completely unnecessary and out of context.

After the club tour, we embarked on a huge production, back to playing in the round with state-of-the-art lasers and moving parts – the stage looked like a spaceship. We started with this show in Australia and, in keeping the same set and themes, then went over to America, where we would play from autumn all the way through to the following spring of 1993.

Then it was back to Europe, to Japan, and back once

more to the United States for another several months. Overall, because the musical landscape had changed worldwide, the reception we got for this wonderful show was not what we expected. All of a sudden it was lame to be an 'entertainer'. All the time that we had spent becoming this great live band that still functioned just like that football team, filling in all the gaps and making sure people got more than their money's worth, seemed like a big waste. Fans were shunning that sort of concert. Now they wanted 'anti-concerts', it seemed, and that's just not what we did. It wasn't in our blood to be sullen and not play to our audiences.

What did we do? Simply soldiered on. That's the English way. Like the bit in Monty Python when the guy loses his arms: 'No worries, it's just a flesh wound.' So we just rolled on, hoping for the best but taking what we got and always working our asses off up there for whoever showed up. It was really expensive to cart all of our stage, lighting and props around – about twelve trucks' worth, not to mention our private plane. It seemed obvious that there was a lack of appreciation for our live set, so we dropped all of the hullabaloo and concentrated on being the kick-ass live band that we always were. Something else happened on this tour that forced us to reconsider the scale of our production: we had a mid-air scare that made us realize that, in addition to being really expensive, a private plane could also be scary as hell.

Two storm fronts hit in St Louis one night while we were

flying through the area in our ten-seat prop plane. We got hit by both of them and dropped 2,000 feet in just seconds. It was pretty scary. Drinks and guitar cases just seemed to float in mid-air before crashing through the toilet door. Thank God everyone was buckled in. Everybody on board was completely silent. We thought this might actually be it – the end of the road. The final curtain. On the hundreds of flights we'd been on together, there had never been anything like this. Everything went deadly quiet. Not a sound from any of us. All of our minds raced to thoughts of Buddy Holly and Lynyrd Skynyrd.

After some very tense moments, thankfully we landed safely. But we were all shaken up enough to say collectively, 'No more planes. Let's just get a bus.' Sav would only really travel on planes from that point on when it was really necessary. The rest of us agreed with Sav, albeit for different reasons. We didn't need a plane any more. If we were stripping down the show, we were also going to strip down our travel.

In addition to the turmoil that we were all feeling with the massive tour, the changing music industry and a changing audience, my marriage was also unfurling. Jacki and I had been drifting apart for a while. She was working more as an actress in New York and Los Angeles while I was travelling the world. That distance just made it harder and harder to maintain a strong relationship. I'd started seeing a woman named Alex, who worked at our record label in

Belgium. We spent time together while the band was on tour. Once the tour ended, however, I ended up breaking up with Alex and trying to make it work at home one more time. But by then Jacki and I had just grown too far apart. Around this time, I started hanging out with Anita, a girl I had met while playing in Michigan and who had recently moved to San Diego. That was the final straw in my relationship with Jacki. We divorced.

I was really good at the music. Juggling relationships, not so much. But I really enjoyed being a dad. Even though I was on the road most of the time, I loved getting to show little Rory the world. I remember him being with us on an American tour when we played in Fargo, North Dakota. One day we had some free time and we found a little coffee shop that had a chess set at one of the tables. We literally sat in there for hours and played chess. He loved it. He had a blast discovering. Normally you wouldn't think of doing something like that, but it was a spur-of-the-moment thing. Something as simple as learning chess was such a big deal to him. Here I was in a position to be able to give my son *stuff* – anything he desired. But right at that moment, he and I were both simply satisfied with having time together.

The *Adrenalize* tour ended in September 1993 after literally hundreds of shows around the world. In the end, *Adrenalize* the album did pretty well. In some countries it actually did better than *Hysteria*, if you can believe that. And it eventually went five times platinum, which is nothing to sneeze at. But on the heels of *Hysteria*, it appeared to have underperformed. It was the glass half-full/half-empty scenario. Five million was amazing, but in the context of our last two albums selling ten million units each, it was viewed as a failure. One thing that it did do was allow us to remain commercially viable, which was important, because the rest of the nineties would get even more challenging for Def Leppard.

Mick Ronson died on 29 April 1993. He was just forty-six years old. A year after Mick died, Joe and I took part in a memorial concert held for him at the Hammersmith Odeon in London. It was an amazing show featuring Roger Taylor from Queen, Roger Daltrey, Bill Nelson from Be-Bop Deluxe, and many others. Ian Hunter was there. I got to play right alongside him. I also played with Trevor Bolder and Woody Woodmansey, the other two original Spiders from Mars. I mean, these were the guys I had seen playing with Bowie in 1973, as a kid watching television, then at Earls Court. They had been the backbone of the Ziggy sound, and they were just as distinctive as they were back when they had on the platform boots and glitter make-up. And they were funny as hell, very droll and comedic, and wonderful storytellers. I remember Woody describing to us how Bowie first approached them about getting all glammed up, these big, tough, burly guys from North Yorkshire. 'Guys,' Bowie told them, 'I want you to wear this.' He had apparently had satin jumpsuits made for the guys, to which

Woody replied in his broad Yorkshire accent, 'I'm not fuckin' wearin' that!' They were appalled at the idea. But ultimately they really got into it once they saw how the girls responded.

Joe and I would be getting to know Trevor and Woody on a whole different level. Including Dick Decent on keyboards, we eventually formed a group of our own with them called the Cybernauts. The Cybernauts toured Japan and actually audio recorded the shows, which we would release on CD several years later. Since Joe and I had both been such huge Bowie freaks since the early seventies, it was really fun getting to know these guys on the road and hearing all of their great stories. We had a few more songs in the can that we recorded in a studio in Dublin. Sadly, Dick Decent, our amazing keyboard player and singer, died in 2011 due to a severe reaction to the antibiotic drug ciprofloxacin, and Trevor Bolder lost his battle with cancer in 2013. Still, we are planning on releasing the songs at some point.

It was time for us to make a new record. The shit we'd got for doing *Adrenalize* actually stung, and, given that our previous record had failed to live up to expectations, we wanted to do something very different. We *had* to do something different. So we decided to change our recording style – from one that screamed 'big production' to something simpler, just as we did with our tour. We also decided to switch up our studio. Instead of renting an expensive recording studio with the latest technology, we rented a quiet villa in southern Spain. It was situated inland from Puerto Banús, a fancy port near Marbella. The weather was amazing and warm – much like that of southern California – and you could see North Africa and Gibraltar from outside the living room, which we'd turned into a temporary studio. Even though we were recording in this villa up in the hills, we were staying in the area of Puerto Banús, where there were upmarket shops and $75 million yachts docked everywhere. Our apartments opened up onto the beach and I had two extra rooms so I could invite my mum and my auntie Grace – my dad's sister – to stay for a visit. They stayed for months. Being that my mum and Grace had spent most of their lives in rainy London, this was like a dream come true for them. They walked around and enjoyed how laid-back everything was. Grace and my mum had never really experienced anything like that. I loved it all and felt really good that they were so at peace. For me, that was everything.

This time Pete Woodroffe was going to produce the album. Pete had been Mike Shipley's assistant on *Adrenalize*. We'd all grown to love his witticisms, tireless work ethic, and open-minded approach to everything, really. Plus he had a very posh British accent.

We were able to incorporate elements of bhangra, Latin percussion, R & B and soul along with rawer guitars and classical East Indian string arrangements on the track 'Turn to Dust' (courtesy of Craig Pruess). We recorded some of the tracks all together, as a pared-down live band in the studio. We had been listening to the recording styles of bands like the Stone Temple Pilots, Soundgarden and Red Hot Chili Peppers, and we wanted to bring that rawness to our sound. This grew into the *Slang* album.

As an artist you're supposed to grow. A lot of our fans want us to write, sing, record and perform the 'same old, same old' and fit into their nostalgic fantasy, but any band should be in a constant state of development or else it will stagnate. Viv was actually very surprised, because he thought that he was in for a classic Def Leppard recording, and we did a complete 180 to what we usually did. People often ask me, 'How have you guys managed to stay together for so long?' Well, first, none of us has let the band or a moment define him. Everyone is much more than that. We didn't want to be defined by what people regarded as our 'sound'. Our goal really was to show people that we made great music that bore our unique brand even if that meant sonically shifting the goal posts to achieve our objective. Listening back to the *Slang* album that was finally released on iTunes, although not our most commercially successful album, I thought it was an extremely creative and essential album for us to do.

For instance, not to get too deep here but take the track 'Breathe a Sigh'. One day, while I was visiting a close friend, I noticed how she looked overwhelmed as she tried to cater to the needs and multiple requests of her husband and her children. Instead of throwing her hands up or even reacting, I briefly saw her breathe a sigh at her predicament. It made me really sad. This story is a theme I've seen many times since and it's beautifully portrayed by Kazuo Ishiguro in his book *The Remains of the Day*, which tells the story of a duty-bound butler letting the love of his life slip between his fingers because of his dedication to the task. As I wrote 'Breathe a Sigh', I didn't want to make it melancholy, so I switched the theme a little and made it about me and Jacki – which actually made it even more melancholy.

It was 1994 and it was turning out to be a year of change for all of us. Sav's dad, Ken Savage, passed away. Sav was the first of us to lose a parent, so we all felt his pain like a bullet, since we were all close not just to our own parents but each other's as well. It was round this time that I began spending time with a gorgeous girl called Anita, who I had previously met in Michigan. Anita was of mixed race. Her mum was black and her biological dad was white. We eventually moved in together. Anita had a bubbly personality and was a lot of fun. She knew all the words to old Motown songs I'd play in the car, which was very impressive, mostly because she hadn't been born when they were released. She actually had a great voice, too.

It took about a year to record *Slang*. But before its release our record label wanted to release a greatest-hits album.

They said they'd prefer it if we had a bonus track as well as the hits. Howard Berman, the head of our British label, Mercury, heard a bunch of demos and loved the song 'When Love and Hate Collide'. So with *Slang* in a slight holding pattern, we recorded the song with Pete Woodroffe in about two weeks, and the *Vault* album was released in 1995, with that single becoming a massive hit in Europe. The album went five times platinum in the US. Due to its content, the album became a huge hit all around the world.

The record label also had the bright idea of having us play three continents in one day, thereby breaking the Guinness World Record. On 23 October 1995, starting at midnight in Tangier, Morocco, we played the first of three acoustic sets that we would play that day. From Africa we flew to London, and then to Vancouver to complete the cycle. And from what I hear, that world record still stands today. It was surreal. It felt like a week because we were in such drastically different environments in such a short space of time. After our gig in a sea cave in Tangier, we were invited to a massive party with belly dancers, camels, soldiers on horses and wonderful Middle Eastern food. We left this party and jumped on a plane to London, where we played at the Shepherd's Bush Empire, located just a few blocks from where my mum lived. We got a chance to see a variety of family and friends, but it was still only ten in the morning. Then we were off to Vancouver to conclude, have a day off, and then leave for a Far East acoustic tour that included

Singapore, Thailand, Indonesia, Australia and Japan.

*Slang* came out in May 1996, and we embarked on a tour that would last the better part of the year. This time out we took a much smaller stage on the road. No more concerts in the round for us. This stage show was far more stripped down, to match the feel of the new album. We started off in Bangkok, worked our way through Korea, Singapore and Japan, and then wound through Europe and the States, with things wrapping up in April 1997. We covered some new ground this time, going to South America and Africa.

Touring South America was a trip. We'd played Mexico before and always maintained that Latin audiences were probably the best on earth (however, the loudest audience we ever experienced was in Montreal). It was more than just touring somewhere where people spoke a different language – the colours and textures of South America seemed different to anywhere else I'd ever been. Rick and I decided to go hang-gliding in Rio on a day off, which we'd never done before. We leapt off a mountain there, glided down and landed on Copacabana Beach. I remember seeing giant butterflies that looked like cartoons. I remember the lush plant life being really green, which is a big deal to me, being colour blind. I'd never seen colours that vivid before. It was also great for Def Leppard to finally get down any-where south of the border. I believe we neglected our huge fan bases in Latin America by spending too much time in the studio. The payoff is that we have made these iconic classic albums. But still, we never seemed to get the time to play in these amazing places. Case in point: when Steve and I went to Australia to do the *Hysteria* album promo, it shot to number one and went double platinum. The album had initially done poorly there. But there just wasn't enough time to do everything and to promote our music to our fans the way we really wanted to.

We finished the entire tour, and I went back to California, where I was now living with my wife-to-be, Anita. By now, Rory was coming to visit me on the weekends, so I'd endure Friday afternoon Los Angeles traffic and pick him up from school, then sit for another few hours in traffic on our way back to Orange County. Still, we found a solution to combat the gridlock. We'd go to a movie, and usually by the time we got out the ride home was a bit more bearable. But I never complained, considering at one point I thought I'd never see my son again. Rory came out on tours, attended recording sessions and travelled with me to Paris, Sweden, Italy and Japan, among other places in the world. Needless to say, my paranoia dissipated. With everything he experienced, world travel and all, I don't think it did for Rory. Children are really fragile, without the thick skin that some of us adults eventually develop. The ones who experience a family break-up are perhaps even more fragile.

I remember going into deep discussions about the subject of children and family within the structure of a touring rock band with one of my closest friends, Scott Smith. Scott was the bass player in the Canadian rock band Loverboy. I'd met him when we toured Europe together in 1987. We'd remained good friends through the years. Sometimes I'd go and stay with Scott and his family in Maple Ridge, Vancouver. Scott was a couple of years older than me and was a reliable source of great advice on business, band life and personal experiences. I'd known Scott and his ex-wife Donna before their break-up. Scott remained in the same house afterward in order to help raise their two boys, Spencer and Brandon, and he and Donna remained the best of friends. I thought it was admirable that Scott would sacrifice his personal life in order to be there for his children. Scott had a talk radio show and sailed a boat. Me and a one-year-old Rory went with Scott and the boys looking for whales one year in the Vancouver islands. We would always end up having these deep philosophical discussions about wives, girlfriends, band idiosyncrasies and band management. It always amazed me how bang on the money he was. Scott was a great help for me in dealing with all of those issues. He had also known me through my relationships with Liz, Jacki and Anita. Each one of them had visited him with me during various stages of my life. Scott's sons loved Anita because she had been in a few hip-hop videos and looked like the trendy girls in the videos they were going gaga over. Scott and I would get a kick out of watching their reaction to her.

*

My auntie Grace died first. She passed away in 1997 on my birthday, 8 December. Auntie Grace never had children, so I was like her little boy. I'd go around to my grandfather's house and my auntie Grace and her husband, Jim, lived with him. We'd go over there every Sunday, it seemed. We were very close. I was kickboxing at Benny 'the Jet' Urquidez's place when I got the news. I came home and called my mum, asking her if she was all right and if she wanted me to come to England for the funeral. She answered, 'Yes.' Auntie Grace's death really freaked her out. They were really close. I flew to England and went to the funeral with my mother. It was interesting because it was my dad's sister with whom my mum had remained close after she and my dad had broken up. But when my auntie Grace got Alzheimer's, my dad was the only person who could really take care of her. She'd phone my dad up and go, 'Ken. Someone stole the bloody keys to the front door.' And he literally would go round and change the locks – stuff like that.

After the funeral, I came back to the States, but my time in California would be short-lived. I got a phone call from Liz on 12 February, saying, 'You had better get your ass back to England quick!' My mother was in the hospital and it wasn't looking good. Liz had been around to visit my mother, as she often did, and my mother started complaining about a stomach ache. Liz immediately took her to the doctor's office, although my mum was going, 'No, no, no. I'm OK,' as they do. The doctor didn't seem to think it was anything very serious. But Liz thought it was something else and took her to the hospital. They kept her and said that it was peritonitis, which is what happens when your appendix bursts and poisons you from the inside. I immediately booked a flight, spoke to my mum, and told her I loved her. My flight wasn't until the next morning, Friday, 13 February, leaving from LAX. Before I left in the morning, I received the news that she had died. Liz held my mother's hand while she passed away, which made me feel better for my mum. I didn't realize how much I'd been dreading this moment until it actually happened and being an only child seemed to make it worse. The worst part of it was that my mum was a very young seventy-two-year-old woman. I felt that she had at least another good twenty years in her, so that's why it was shocking. Ironically, as I was waiting for my car service to take me to LAX, I came up with the guitar riff for the song 'Promises'.

When I got to England, there was much to do. I'd never had to do anything like that before. Liz helped a lot, and she was great. The constant phone calls and then having to arrange a funeral were almost overwhelming. Liz and I have always been close, and I am thankful she was there for me during that time.

After everything was said and done, I flew back home to California. I was there for a while until ultimately another trip to England came up. I wasn't really looking forward to going, since it would be my first time back without my mum. I decided to rent a Winnebago sleeper van and take Rory and Anita to southern England to see some castles. This was just the ticket. We all had a blast visiting places like Corfe Castle and Dorset, Devon and Cornwall. My dad had taken us in his sleeper van when I was a kid. This was summer in England, and it was cool. In hindsight, I figure the following: when someone important to you dies, you put everything on hold. It was a subconscious decision, but I removed myself from life for a moment. To me, I pressed a reset button, and it helped me deal with the stress. I think if you struggle with that notion, then you run into frustrations. The more experienced you become, the less you worry about everything. What would have been crippling years ago you now brush off. In the grand scheme of things, most things are trivial pursuits. Things like career, popularity, etc. all have less of a stranglehold.

It was 1998 and we had started recording the *Euphoria* album in Dublin at Joe's place. Pete Woodroffe produced the album and Mutt would be involved in the songwriting and recording process again. He did four songs, 'It's Only Love', 'All Night', 'Guilty' and 'Promises'. Around the same time, a terrible terrorist bombing occurred in Omagh, Northern Ireland. One Saturday afternoon a splinter group called the Real IRA, opposing the IRA's ceasefire, planted a car bomb that went off prematurely, killing twenty-nine people – Protestants and Catholics alike, including six teenagers and a woman pregnant with twins – and wounding hundreds of others. The band was in Southern Ireland at the time. It wasn't that far away. It was really a horrible event, and when we heard about it the song seemed to write itself and wound up being 'Paper Sun'.

I think *Euphoria* is very underrated sonically and structurally. I played it recently and was shocked at how great it sounded. We bypassed the raw approach that we had applied to the *Slang* album and went overboard on the backing vocals. I think we did some ludicrous amount of multi-tracking, and I actually love the way it sounds. Also, at this point, music was moving into another era, everyone having got bored with the whole grunge rock antihero thing. Bursting onto the scene were entertainer/pop acts like Britney Spears, Backstreet Boys, *NSYNC, etc. It was OK to use massive light shows and have fun again. I've always been humbled that we managed to maintain a career during all the changes while keeping our integrity. All of a sudden we were actually cool again. At a festival we did with the band Hole, someone yelled out, 'Def Leppard sucks!' because the guitar player in Hole was wearing a Def Leppard T-shirt. Courtney Love actually retorted back something like, 'Show some respect! Def Leppard is an amazing band!'

Funnily enough, as I began to feel less and less controlled by the industry I was in, I received a phone call from Peter Mensch. He called to tell me that because *Hysteria* was in an exclusive little club of its own by going over ten times platinum – meaning it had now sold in excess of ten million copies in the US alone – we would be receiving an invitation to the first Diamond Award ceremony. This club is a very special one. The Diamond Award was created by the Recording Industry Association of America (RIAA) to honour sales of ten million copies or more of an album or single. The ceremony was held on 16 March 1999, in New York City, at the Roseland Ballroom. At the time, there were only sixty-eight artists who had achieved this status. Among that group were Michael Jackson, Elton John, Prince, the Beatles, Led Zeppelin, us and not that many more. This was actually *very* special. People often ask, 'At what point did you realize you'd made it or achieved what you set out to do?' The real moment for me was when I gave up my thirty-quid-a-week job to become a professional musician. But I think everyone likes to hear the more glamorous answer, which would probably be, 'When I stood on that podium and took up the microphone to say thank you along with my bandmates and the guys from Metallica,' then seeing who was in the audience – Elton John, Jimmy Page, Billy Joel, etc. and realizing they were our peers. We've never been considered for a Grammy Award and weren't really trendy enough to get that par-ticular recognition, but we made great records. A couple of years later we would get another Diamond Award. The reason the huge success of the band wasn't apparent to me before, apart from having a lot of the personal stuff happening that past year, was because we were usually either making a record or touring, and I really never used the time to reflect.

The *Euphoria* album was released in early 1999 and the single 'Promises' was actually a minor hit, as was the album, which went gold. I remember once the album came out, we all went on *The Howard Stern Show* in New York. I remember how shocked Howard was that we weren't as crazy and debauched as he'd heard. It really kind of proved how those rumours have taken hold. He was talking about the in-the-round under-stage orgies that we'd all been hearing about for years. Unfortunately, someone forgot to involve us in them.

We started touring America in June 1999 and continued all through the summer. In the autumn, we went through Japan and Europe, returning to America in December. During a short break I finally got married to Anita on 17 December, in Laguna Beach, California, near our home. But then it was back out on the road. On 31 December, we played our Y2K show at the Rosemont Horizon in Chicago. It was a fantastic gig that we'd done many times before. When it hit midnight, the world didn't end and aliens didn't swoop down from the lighting rig, so we carried on with the tour.

Apart from a few amazing shows, the record industry was really changing. The advent of the internet made the recording and publishing industry as we knew it borderline obsolete. Record sales were declining 8 per cent each year due to the downloading of music, illegal or otherwise. But, more interestingly, it created an environment of 'free ownership', where people just didn't invest in or buy music any more.

We also got into a bit of a rut playing state fairs. It started getting a little bit frustrating. We were still valid and better than ever onstage, but we were playing these really shitty venues. Despite everyone telling us how great we were, we didn't seem to have much to show for it. I really wanted us to get independent PR and have a much stronger presence on the internet, which had finally put the world in a stranglehold. Although our record label promised us many things, we felt that they didn't really deliver. We had felt that we had run our course with our management, Q Prime, and that it was time for a change. They had worked with us for a long time. But now it was time to move on. They had other clients. It was getting frustrating because we felt that we were not the priority we once had been. As occurs in any progressing relationship, we reached a crossroads. We needed a fresh approach.

This all came to a head after we played in front of 12,000 rabid fans in a field by a river somewhere in the Midwest. I threw a wobbler at the band. I said, 'Fuck! I don't want to do this any more. I don't want to sit here and just watch all of this disappear when we obviously have people who love us but we're doing absolutely nothing to push ourselves forward.' Everyone in the band said, 'Well, we're with you, whatever you want to do.' I told them I thought we should change management. We eventually did, in 2005.

As everything was switching over to digital, major record labels tried to scramble together and circle the wagons: they started releasing their artists' albums digitally. However, because of Mensch and Burnstein's masterstroke, our label wasn't allowed to do that. They had put a clause in our recording contract stating that the label couldn't release on an alternate medium without the band's explicit consent. It was a godsend: otherwise we'd have ended up in court alongside Eminem and countless others, having been taken advantage of by the big, bad corporate record companies who offered the same royalty rate for digital format as for the physical format, even though costs were much lower. In short, Q Prime gave us control of our future. Also luckily for us, Def Leppard had managed to become entrenched in pop culture, albeit in a slightly nostalgic way. All the things we had achieved and endured through the years made us compelling subject matter – poster boys for survival and perseverance. So much so that the cable network VH1 made our story one of their first episodes in the documentary series *Behind the Music* in 1998. The documentary was well received, and it helped revive us to a degree, because the network would re-air the crap out of it.

I also should mention that it was at this time when I was at home on a break during the *Euphoria* tour, that Greg Ladanyi, famed American record producer (Fleetwood Mac, Don Henley, Jackson Browne, etc.), said to me, 'This is someone you should meet.' He then introduced me to C. J. Vanston, who had played on a gazillion records as a keyboard player and who was also a producer. We hit it off and went in many different directions with writing. It could be country, pure pop or even a soul song. This started a relationship between C. J. and me that has endured to this day. C. J. ended up co-writing with me the Def Leppard song 'All About Believin'' on the *Mirrorball* album.

I was up at C. J.'s place when a toilet valve broke at my house in Laguna Hills, taking out the bathroom upstairs and in turn the kitchen below via the ceiling, and every room in its wake. I walked through the door and the alarm was going off. My poor German Shepherd dog Woofie started howling as all this water was pouring from the ceiling. This was more than an inconvenience, as I had to eventually move out of the house for about a six- or seven-month period while it was being repaired. I temporarily moved into this lovely house in Laguna Beach. Once I settled in, I remember getting a phone call from Scott. He said he was sailing down from Vancouver and that he'd stop off and see me in either Newport Beach or Dana Point, two harbours that were very close to Laguna. However, he never made it. I later received a phone call from his ex-wife

Donna, who told me that he'd disappeared overboard in San Francisco Bay. Everyone was still combing the area looking for him. Apparently a freak wave had knocked the boat on its side. When the boat turned back over, Scott was nowhere to be seen. Mike Reno, Loverboy's lead singer, spent the next two days frantically searching for Scott, but unfortunately he was never found. This was like when my mum had died. I wasn't ready for her to go. Yet here I was again, speaking to someone on the phone, making plans to see them, and then somehow getting the news that they had died. Like my mum and Steve, Scott went way before his time, and I felt cheated. I can only imagine how his family felt because Scott was such a loved person.

In 2001, we got ready to head over to Joe's studio at his home in Dublin, dubbed 'Joe's Garage'. By this time, we would all have been working on some ideas for the new album in our respective homes and then bringing those ideas together to work on them, rather than starting from scratch like we did in the old days.

We decided to call the album *X* (ten) because technically it was the tenth album for Def Leppard (I had joined up with them on number three). We worked with Pete Woodroffe again as a producer, and this time out in terms of concept we decided to sort of go the 'pop' route.

For the first time ever, our record label also suggested that we record a song that had already been written by someone else, in this case a guy named Wayne Hector, which was kind of a strange thing for us. But we played along with it. I think they suggested it to get some new blood in the room; they were just looking for a hit, and so were we. Marti Frederiksen, who had produced a lot of latter-day Aerosmith, came in to work with us as well. We had our guard up with these strangers at first, but they were great and the experience was better than we expected. But during this time a couple of things happened.

My most faithful companion of the past ten years had been my dog Woofie. I got her when she and Rory were both six months old. She was a constant throughout my time in Laguna Hills. So it was heartbreaking when I got the phone call from Anita. Woofie had been sick, but now she had taken a turn for the worse. She had cancer. About a week after I got to Joe's place in Dublin, where I was recording the album, Anita phoned and told me that she couldn't get Woofie into the car. So I called Stan Schiller, my friend and then guitar tech, who came to the house to help her. They took Woofie to the vet. By the time they arrived, Woofie was so weak the vets told Anita, 'We should put her down.' I had to give the authorization over the phone. I felt bad, but I felt worse for Anita because she had to endure it all alone.

The bulk of 2001 was taken up with recording until the day that changed everything.

On 11 September 2001, I remember seeing the events

unfold on TV like everyone else and was still unclear as to why, how and what was going on. The next day I was in an elevator in Los Angeles and total strangers were talking to each other. They were talking about President George W. Bush's speech and his thoughts on the terrorists' motives: 'They hate us for our freedom.' The people in the elevator seemed to buy this explanation. I, however, needed a lot more – I just couldn't comprehend why fifteen Saudi Arabian nationals would commit suicide and mass murder in such a dramatic fashion. I began reading and researching to help me understand more. I'd never cared too much for politics, but this event changed me. I saw the noted philosopher and political commentator Noam Chomsky basically get thrown off a TV talk show because he was trying to explain why he thought this event had occurred. So obviously I started devouring all of his books. This led to other authors, such as Howard Zinn and Australian journo John Pilger, and new political discoveries, which gave me an alternative understanding to what we, the general masses, had been fed on a daily basis for many years. The fact that fifteen Saudis attacked America, which responded by invading Afghanistan, whereby a faction of the US public responded by buying gas masks and duct tape, fearing a biological attack from the former puppet dictator of Iraq, Saddam Hussein, who'd ignored his script and attacked Kuwait, was interesting to say the least. The more I read, the more I saw a familiar pattern emerging:

history seemed to be repeating itself over and over again, identically, with every imperial empire making the same mistakes. It almost seemed like the movie *The Matrix*, and almost everyone else had swallowed the blue pill and was delightfully floating along in blissful ignorance. This was an awakening for me in that I was starting to pay more attention to the world beyond just the musical bubble I lived in. At this point, I couldn't believe that I had been travelling around the world and had not been aware of any of this. It was like when I went back to London after a tour in my late thirties or early forties and 'saw' the architecture that I'd grown up around for years for the first time. The realization of the beauty around me was a powerful one and almost brought me to tears. To this day, when I go to a beautiful city like Paris or Prague, I truly appreciate what I see on such a different level. The most wondrous part of my transformation was that when I actually conversed with someone whom I would never have met had I not been in a world-touring band, I could actually have an experience and conversation on such a level that I would not have believed possible. Within the same year on two very different occasions I had a conversation with the Queen of England and an arms dealer, however brief. I can remember when Def Leppard played the Jubilee concert in Leeds, England. We met the Queen after our performance. She was as sharp as a razor blade as she shifted gears talking to everybody in line. You can't unlearn stuff like this. It affects every other aspect of your life. A lot of things start making sense. So, like I said, I had all of these amazing experiences with amazing people, and yet my intellect had still not been activated. What unfolded in the aftermath of 11 September activated my intellect. As a result, my learning and awareness curve started spiking at a ferocious pace.

Although we had only recently got married, we had previously been together for about five or six years. The first few years of being together before we were married were harmonious and lovely. As the relationship continued, a few cracks began to appear. Still, in spite of what little things might have occurred, we tied the knot. But instead of getting closer, we actually drifted further apart, no matter how hard we tried to fix things – so much so that we began to live separate lives in separate homes. With my house in ruins, Anita started spending more time in our condo in LA, and I was spending more time at the rental in Laguna Beach. I realized having all this deep philosophical knowledge that I was acquiring actually didn't make my real-life situations any better because I wasn't really using any of it. Around this time I started seeing a new girlfriend, Michele, since Anita and I were off-again, on-again, although technically I was still married. I had actually become my dad, so to speak. Not that my dad was having those kinds of relationships with women in his life, but he was definitely exhausted trying to please and look after everyone to the point of neglecting himself.

I was also paying more attention to my dad. After twenty or so years of my being in Def Leppard, my almost eighty-year-old father had a proposition for me. Could he come out on the road and travel with us for a bit? He had faced some difficult times recently. Auntie Grace and my mother had died, and my dad's girlfriend, Doris, whom he had lived with for the past twenty-five years, had also passed away. All of a sudden he was on his own. He also asked me for the only thing he'd ever asked for – a caravan/trailer that would become his home. So I bought him a caravan. He was ecstatically happy. He would park up and camp out in various campgrounds around the country. I felt he seemed truly liberated. He could read and drink tea, all on his own time.

One really funny incident happened when he was parked up in a field just outside Brighton. He noticed that there seemed to be a lot of activity in the next field over. Some of the people said they were having a Christmas party. They felt sorry for my dad and invited him over, but they warned him that they were 'naturalists'. My dad thought that meant they were 'hippie tree-huggers' but soon found out they were without clothing. It was a nudist colony. The amazing thing was my dad soon found himself without clothing, too. Although he didn't consider himself a naturalist, he had no problem with being stark, bollock naked. This whole period for my dad was what I like to call 'The Liberation of Ken'. I was so happy for him. We shifted to a higher phase of our relationship. He was so happy that all of a sudden he had no commitments. He even left the house in Holland Park, London (which I had originally bought my mum in 1989), to chill in his caravan. My dad also came out on the road with us for the X tour in the summer of 2002. And having been a truck driver his whole life, he loved being on a truck or a bus or anything like that, so being on the road seemed to really be like home for him. He would often ride up front, talking to the driver, swapping shop stories about what it was like to drive for a living. One day our tour bus broke down at a roundabout in West London. The bus rolled back into a wall and wouldn't move, so we all got out and pushed. I was pissing myself laughing as everyone watched my dad and Rick Allen trying to push this bus. We ditched the bus and walked about a mile to the Hammersmith Odeon, where we headlined a show that night.

On the X tour, I'd hang with my dad as much as I could. We had a ball. After it wrapped up in late 2003, he stayed with us for a bit in California. I remember Anita, Rory and I took my dad to Las Vegas to see a Cirque du Soleil show, and he reacted almost the same way Rory did when he was just a young boy, as if he was witnessing real magic. It was great to see my dad enjoying life – and he was hanging with his only grandchild, too. Three generations of Collen men, having a good time – priceless.

All was well with my dad until I got a phone call from

Liz, who had been taking my dad to his doctor visits. This time she said, 'I think you should come home.' This was weird because we had been here before with my mum. Liz was great. Once again she took on the burden. I got the news that my dad had two months to live. He had pancreatic cancer. Now it all became clear why my dad had been complaining about stomach aches about six months earlier. I dropped everything and travelled from LA to London.

In the midst of all this, my romantic life was getting full-on complicated again. I found out that Michele was pregnant and I'd have to break the news to everyone. I'd been selfishly, narcissistically juggling relationships and was hurting all the wonderful people around me, but, on top of that, my dad was physically fading as cancer got the upper hand, so that became my immediate focus. He was razor sharp and we had some of the best conversations of our lives. Yet the role reversal between my dad and me was interesting. I'd never thought I'd be in the position of having to care for an ailing parent. It was very different from when my mum died because then I'd been out of the country. Liz was there with my mum to take the brunt of the weight and was there for my dad as well. But I'm so glad I got to spend the time that I did with my dad.

The British healthcare system was wonderful to my dad. They sent a nurse round to help bathe and shave him. They supplied special beds and all sorts of stuff. I was always on hand. I'd go to the pharmacy and wherever I was needed.

At one point he was in hospital in Fulham, London, and Liz and I would visit him. One day I came in and noticed that the bed opposite my dad was empty. Its previous occupant had been an old Indian man who was in pain and obviously suffering. Now he was gone. My dad said, 'Can you take me home? I don't want to be here any more.' So I took him home to the house in Holland Park, where my dad and I spent the last months of his life together. My dad was about eighty-one years old then, and it was funny how he had never really stopped growing as a person. We would sit at home and I would give my dad his morphine treatments and we would have these great conversations about life. In all honesty, one of the happiest times for my dad was after all the women in his life had died. Now don't get me wrong. I don't wish death upon anyone, and I know that's a pretty strong admission, but I get it. My dad was certainly devastated that everyone had passed on, but sitting butt naked without a care in a field drinking tea alone wasn't such a bad alternative. These are the sort of things I spoke to my dad about in his last days, and we couldn't help but laugh our asses off at the seriousness and the epiphany of what one discovers on one's deathbed.

It was so hot that summer – very unlike most British summers. I had a fan going and all the windows open. My dad would get tired a lot and sleep, so I put a baby monitor in his room. Rory and Anita came over to visit, which he loved very much. I'm really glad my son had a chance to spend that kind of time with his granddad. A lot of my family got a chance to say their farewells directly to my dad during this time period – his brother Eric, my cousin Elaine, her husband Bart, and their two children Leah and Joe, Elaine's sister Judy, and many good friends like Rudi and Simon. My dad passed away on 31 July 2004. I missed him slipping away. A doctor was in the house, who woke me up and said my dad had gone. I guess that was the weird part, with him being so alive in that state, and then all of a sudden he wasn't there any more. I can remember that while waiting for the ambulance to show up I closed my dad's eyes. I had an odd feeling about not having my parents here any more – there was a feeling of being orphaned, like I now had to be the adult in charge.

Joe flew over from Dublin for the funeral, but he went to the wrong funeral home. Odd coincidence: the funeral director there happened to be the brother of Steve Priest, bass player from the Sweet, a seventies glam-rock band Joe and I loved. He recognized Joe and told him who he was. Joe was interested to hear that, but he was also stressed that he was about to miss my dad's funeral. The director told Joe in a posh British accent, 'You'd better hurry. The funeral starts in twenty-five minutes and it's an hour away.' Joe made it. He didn't catch the whole service, but he did arrive before it ended, rushing in and making an entrance like only Joe can do.

I buried my dad's ashes at the City of London Cemetery

near Wanstead, East London, a day after my daughter Samantha was born. I'd been in Germany the night before, doing a TV show with Def Leppard. I called Michele at the hospital in Anaheim, California. Michele said, 'It's a girl and she's got bright red hair.' This shocked the hell out of me. Although I didn't actually get to see for myself until two weeks later, when I returned to California, her hair was indeed bright red, very much like my mum's. I didn't expect Samantha to have my mum's hair. I was delighted. After Samantha was born, Michele and I called a truce on our relationship and I tried to make my marriage work with Anita. Eventually, amazingly, Anita and Michele sat down together and helped work things out with me to create as comfortable a situation as we could have for Samantha (whom Anita wound up adoring, by the way). Unfortunately, it was too late to fix my relationship with Anita, so although we didn't divorce immediately, we split up after a few months. With all of that going on, it was a bit complicated when I started yet another relationship with a girl I met named Kamilah.

Before my dad passed, during the time I was taking care of him in London, I had a chance to reconnect with some old friends. Simon Laffy, my former Girl bass player, would come over and see my dad and we always got to talking about music. Liz had played me some demos by him and was really impressed. Simon and I had never really written songs together when we were in Girl, but we had always appreciated the same types of obscure music – from dub reggae and fusion jazz rock to full-on punk. So we started writing songs, two of which in particular I remember being pretty good. I remember saying to Simon, 'Wouldn't Paul Cook from the Sex Pistols be perfect on these songs?' Two days later, I had a meeting with my dad's doctor. As I left, I saw Paul Cook getting into a car, somewhere in Chelsea, not far from where my dad was staying in hospital. That was strange, I thought. I'd known Paul to say hello to for years – in London, musicians constantly bump into each other – but who would have thought I would run into him outside a hospital?

'Your ears must've been burning,' I said, and told him about the music Simon and I had been making and asked him if he'd like to come down and rehearse. He said, 'Sure.' And that's how Manraze was born.

The three members of Manraze (being myself, Paul Cook and Simon Laffy) were really getting excited over the sound we were creating. We had absolutely no restrictions musically. We were all huge fans of soul, Motown and sixties reggae, along with punk, rock and whatever kind of music tickled our fancy. After the first few times we played, it became apparent that being in a three-piece band was a liberating experience. You could go off on musical excursions without sticking to the structures of four- or five-piece bands. We really got into the concept of the classic three-piece bands like the Jimi Hendrix Experience and the Police.

The music we created seemed to bear their trademarks. So we started playing small gigs. This was strange for a number of reasons. I can remember standing amongst the drum cases after our first ever show at the Spitz club in East London. We let Jeni, Paul's wife, sit in the passenger seat. It was a real déjà vu throwback to when we first started playing in bands. We didn't have management or road crew taking care of everything. The other thing was that I would be singing lead vocals. The singing part was not a problem, as I've been singing since I was a kid and for years doing backing vocals with Def Leppard, but with the main focus being on my guitar playing. This was completely different. I had to change the plan a little bit because all of a sudden the guitar playing had to take a back seat, since I had to focus on the singing part first. Add on top of that, I'm the classic lyric forgetter. Many a night I've hummed and mumbled, Bob Dylan style, through classic Def Leppard songs, even ones I've written. Now I was faced with singing lead vocals without three other great singers to hide behind. I was still playing lead guitar, but I'd have to sing first, relying on lyric sheets scattered about the floor. The first year of shows was interesting, to say the least, but amazing fun and great energy. I'm not sure if anyone actually noticed that I was singing the wrong words.

We recorded our first album, *Surreal*, at Joe's studio in Dublin with Ger McDonnell engineering and producing. It was a fiery stew of all the influences we never got a chance to pay homage to in our other bands. You could definitely hear the Clash, the Pistols, the Police, Hendrix, and even bands like Nirvana and Linkin Park thrown in there. It may not have lit a huge fire commercially, but it was as artistically fulfilling as almost anything else I'd done up until that point. That's what mattered. We were creating a great musical hybrid, blending differing styles of music into one new sound, and I was revelling in it.

In 2005 I had some time off, so I decided to go to India in either March or April with Kamilah. Def Leppard was gearing up to release a second greatest-hits album, a double best-of called *Rock of Ages*. I think because the industry had started to slow down, everyone was feeling it, so record labels started circling the wagons and releasing more albums by established bands. It was becoming a crap time to be a new band on the scene unless you had a super buzz or optimum support from a label. Q Prime suggested we tour. It would be a double-headliner act, with us and Canadian rocker Bryan Adams. Initially, a pairing like this would have seemed out of context, although we'd played with Bryan in the past, but the inspiration for this type of tour was when Bob Dylan and Willie Nelson went out as a package to rave reviews and packed houses. It was the 'one plus one equals three' theory. This concept of double billing prevails and even dominates to this day. It's become essential. Even really big artists go out on the same tour as opposed to the old headline-and-support-act combo.

This tour was to be played in minor-league baseball stadiums across America. Although it was a good tour, I still had the feeling we could be doing a lot better. This was also the first tour we'd ever done that was not promoting an original album, which always bothered Joe because he didn't want us to become a nostalgia act relying on the hits of yesteryear.

As the industry was moving in a whole new direction, we felt it was time for a change. Coincidentally, a friend of mine named Gavin introduced me to Trudy Green, who was from the UK and managed Aerosmith along with her then business partner Howard Kaufman. After meeting with Howard, it became clear that an association with Trudy and Howard should be the new direction for Def Leppard. Howard's and Trudy's ideas were a lot different to what we had been doing for the past few years. Now it was down to convincing the rest of the guys this was the way forwards. That was a slow process. No one in Def Leppard is good with change. There were some obvious things that we weren't doing and Howard brought logic into the situation and handled things accordingly. I'm not sure if it was at the end of or during the tour, but we eventually made the switch from Q Prime to HK Management, which was definitely the right move at this point in our career.

Trudy's assistant was Mike Kobayashi. Mike is half Thai, half Japanese, and 100 per cent American, meaning one time we were in Tokyo (although Mike looks like a local) people would talk to him in English, skipping any native tongue. Mike is super smart, super rational, very hip and up on everything. On top of that, he's one of the nicest guys I've ever met. Although the band would later part ways with Trudy Green, we would still remain under the care of Howard Kaufman. Luckily, Mike would make that switch with us. We pretty much talk to each other almost every day. Mike handles most of our business and is involved in every aspect of our careers. For me that includes Def Leppard, Manraze and Delta Deep (which I'll talk about a little later). In 2006, the first tour we did with HK was to support *Yeah!*, an album of cover tunes by bands that influenced the Def Leppard sound. Our only boundaries were that they couldn't be Beatles, Stones, Zeppelin or Queen. And even though we covered Bowie and T. Rex songs, they were deep cuts, not breakout hits by those artists. We wanted to keep it a little subtle, leaving some people to think they were original songs. Howard suggested, for the 2006 tour to support that album, we should go out with Journey. He said, 'Trust me. I think it will be huge.' We weren't convinced, but all that changed on the first date of the tour in Camden, New Jersey, when all 23,000 tickets were sold and 3,000 people couldn't get in. The tour was a raging success, and Journey was awesome. They were so good it really inspired us to raise our own bar every night. On that tour I met Scotty Appleton, who was Neal Schon's guitar tech. Our next tour after the Journey tour I was without a tech and Scott was without a tour, so it all worked out perfectly, especially since Scott is such a lovely guy. He defies any tech stereotypes . . . except for being a guitar geek. He's got a wine collection and is also a great photographer.

SCOTT APPLETON: I first met Phil on the 2006 Def Leppard/Journey tour. I was working for Neal Schon of Journey at the time and was really enjoying watching the Leppard guys play after we finished our load-outs. I was sitting backstage by the crew room one afternoon after the Def Leppard sound check, playing a Thorn guitar that I had on the road with me. Phil came down the hallway and looked at the guitar and said 'WHAT IS THAT??!!' I explained that a friend of mine had built the guitar and he asked if he could try it out. A few minutes later we were onstage and had it plugged into his rig, blasting away. All he could say was, 'I LOVE the feel of this neck!!' The neck on the guitar is quite large, and I think I may have turned Phil into a 'big neck' fan that day, as the ones on his guitars have been getting progressively larger every year. So fast-forward to 2007. Journey decided to take a year off and I was looking for a gig, and I got a call from the Def Leppard guys. Phil needed a guitar tech. I jumped at the chance and flew to Los Angeles to start rehearsals. As with any gig, there is a bit of a learning curve when you start, not only new equipment but new personalities as well. I was learning all the programme changes during rehearsals and didn't have all of them quite placed properly, and Phil was so cool about it. He never once was frustrated or flew off the handle. I honestly thought I was going to get fired because 'this guy can't possibly be this nice'. Working with Phil is a blast because we both are guitar geeks at heart. We are always looking for a way to improve upon what we have already done and push the envelope a little further. Not to mention that we are always laughing, and have built a level of trust with each other so that it is a no-stress environment. It's always a joy to work with one of your best friends.

During the Journey tour, we played the Hollywood Bowl. It being LA meant that backstage was filled with celebrities. We got word that Tim McGraw was going to be there. Rick Allen knew Tim because his brother, Robert, had worked with Tim and his wife, Faith Hill. Tim had always mentioned to Rick that he loved Def Leppard and that it would be great one day to do a song together. Since I knew that, I started noodling around with an idea of what a song would sound like if Def Leppard fused with Tim McGraw. Within ten seconds of meeting him, I started humming this idea, and he said, 'Yeah! And we could have a stop section there! And this is where Joe comes in . . . !' And before you know it we had most of the song done right there and then in a crowded hallway in the Hollywood Bowl. This song would end up being called 'Nine Lives'. I love it when that happens. It wouldn't be completed for another year, but it ended up on *Songs from the Sparkle Lounge* and on one of Tim's greatest-hits albums, too.

Speaking of country music, we did this show called *Crossroads* with Taylor Swift. At the time, Taylor was just blowing up. We'd read in *Rolling Stone* that this young superstar wanted to do *Crossroads* with us because we were one of her favourite bands. In 2008 we went out to Nashville and added Taylor and her band to about five of our songs and vice versa, making for a cacophony of country and rock. The really interesting thing to me was that a lot of Taylor's songs were constructed in the vein of another one of her favourite artists – Shania Twain. Ironically, we recognized Mutt Lange's influence, as he'd written a lot of the songs with Shania, his then wife, thus completing the circle so that a lot of our songs fit together seamlessly. Although nothing really came of the experience for us, with the exception of a hard-to-find DVD, we all had a great time making great music together.

At the end of the 2006 *Sparkle Lounge* tour with Journey, I splashed out and finally bought my dream car – a metallic meteorite-grey Aston Martin DB9. I've always had a sincere fascination with cars. I love the look of them. That image was probably my earliest appreciation of art without even realizing it. The lines, the curves and colours all wrapped around harnessed horsepower waiting to be unleashed. I think my earliest memory of wanting a specific car was in the sixties after seeing *Goldfinger* with Sean Connery as James Bond zooming around in a totally pimped-out Aston Martin DB5 equipped with machine guns, the capacity to produce an oil slick and an ejector seat.

This James Bond fascination finally got to me. My Aston didn't have an ejector seat, but it was a convertible, which was even better, as I wouldn't really take anyone in the car that I wanted to chuck out. The DB9 was my absolute dream car, but with it there was a huge letdown. The car was beautiful, sexy-ass and fast, but the romantic idea of freedom, independence and escapism wasn't there any more. It was back in the old Ford Escort van I'd owned in the seventies, which I'd slept in, shagged in and done pretty much everything else in. That was living the dream. Phil Lewis once said, 'Freedom is a full tank of gas!' and he was bang on.

When I was growing up, cars had names that seemed to reflect a working-class image. But for me, cars such as the Viva, the Cortina and the Morris Minor eventually got replaced by those with flashier names like Diablo, Vanquish and Gallardo, and numbers such as M3, GT3 and 918. Cars have always been part of rock star/famous person folklore and are seen in some cases as proof of having made it. A flash motor has always had the association with hot, tasty-looking chicks and impressing anyone who happens to glance your way, letting them know immediately that they're looking at someone special. They are also the dream of boys and men of all ages.

But with all that said, it's not about the car – it's about the experience in the car. Cars can represent escapism, speed or a personal rocket ship. But the idea of a car for me symbolized real independence, and the happiest I have ever been was in my simpler, pedal-to-the-metal mediocrities. I can honestly say that the best times I've ever had in cars were the early years of driving those very humble and modest working-class motors, or when I drove a rented car. I've had every kind of luxury car you could imagine. I've driven them all. But when you remove all of the spit and shine I've come to realize that it isn't about the package. It's about the ride. And I've had some of my best rides in a car you wouldn't look twice at. Case in point, recently I had the most spectacular experience when I drove with my wife Helen and our friend Debbi Blackwell-Cook to a place called Paradise on the South Island of New Zealand in a rented Toyota. I wish I'd figured this out sooner before spending a fortune on Porsches, Mercedes, Beamers and Jags over the years.

I've ultimately come to the conclusion that it's the freedom, especially when coupled with youthful discovery, that has ended up being important to me. Don't get me wrong: I still really dig and appreciate those fine cars, but

I'd never let a car define me. As I'm writing this, I just got back from driving my twelve-year-old BMW X5 (in perfect condition, with 131,000-plus miles) to the beach. My dog Shaq was in the back, with sand everywhere. We basically had a two-hour vacation. This car is older than my oldest daughter, Samantha. Even though I feel deliciously wooed every time I see a new X6 M, I happen to just really like my X5 and I'm loath to get rid of it or replace it with a newer model. That's saying a lot for a guy who used to buy a new car every three years, like I did. I am glad that I finally sussed this out because it's been bothering me for years. I have been looking for the dots to connect ever since I had that afternoon flash point in my black Porsche on Blackfriars Bridge in London years ago.

Near the end of 2007 (by which time I was fully separated from Anita), I met Shawyana one day at the beach. We had a good time together and enjoyed working out along with exploring health and fitness regimens. We became close pretty quickly, and soon she and her seven-year-old son Nico were living with me at my house in Laguna Hills. Plus she could cook her ass off. In 2008, Def Leppard embarked upon a fairly extensive tour outside of the US, visiting all of the places that we had neglected for a while and some places that we had never been before. This was to further promote the *Sparkle Lounge* album that we'd started promoting in 2006 on the US tour with Journey.

While we were on tour the Sparkle Lounge was a room where Dave Wolff, Vivian's guitar tech, would faithfully place guitar amps and sparkly Christmas lights in the hope that we'd get our rock on in there. Of course we never did, but he'd set it up every day anyway. We decided that we could start recording a new album whilst on tour. That's what Greg Ladanyi had done with Jackson Browne many years previously, and it had turned out to be Jackson's biggest album. We really needed to find the time, so every effort was made to at least start some of these songs for a new album. We'd set up an electronic drum kit and practise combo amps. We actually did get some stuff done – 'Nine Lives' was one of the songs started on tour. In fact, I did my backing vocals on the chorus in a bathroom while Journey were blasting away onstage. Ronan McHugh, our house sound engineer, who'd become the band's producer on the *Yeah!* album, recorded everything. We thought that we'd actually redo it properly at some point, but when I got to do it at a real studio, it sounded like crap compared to the bathroom session. Ironic, that. So we used the bathroom vocals. This is why we called the album *Songs from the Sparkle Lounge*.

The tour took us to Eastern Europe, including Lithuania and Turkey, Russia and Greece. A lot of these places we toured with David Coverdale and his band Whitesnake, who were always a hoot. I always got on great with David. He made a special guest appearance on the Delta Deep debut album – a band I formed years later – where he performed on 'Private Number'. The tour wound through the States and Canada, and concluded with some Japanese and Australian dates, finally wrapping up in New Zealand in November 2008. I always liked playing Australia since I could reconnect with my cousin Georgie and his wife, Mary, and daughter, Claire. I also fell in love with New Zealand. I ended up buying a house there.

For me, 2009 was a serious year. In the midst of my relationship with Shawyana, my on-again, off-again relationship with Kamilah gave me my second daughter, Savannah, who was born in Alexandria, Virginia. (We would later also have another daughter, Charlotte.) In 2008 in Reading, Pennsylvania, during our tour with Styx, I had briefly met Helen Simmons, who would eventually become my wife. Helen was from Brooklyn, New York. In 2009 she was our official VIP hostess for Live Nation – the tour operators and promoters. This basically meant in each city she organized the backstage fan experience along with great seats and a party that included food, drinks and a meet-and-greet.

That year we also started rehearsing for part two of the *Sparkle Lounge* tour in Dublin. The big thing for Def Leppard was that we were to headline the Download Festival in Donington, the same place where Rick Allen had made his triumphant return to the stage twenty-three years previously. Manraze was also to play Download the day before Def Leppard. While in Dublin, I would do double duty. I'd rehearse in the afternoon with Def Leppard, drive across town and then rehearse with Manraze at night.

The day of Def Leppard's Download performance, the weather was beautiful and picture perfect. We've played it since, and it has pissed down rain, as is usually the case with British festivals. It was a career highlight. There were 80,000 people there, we played great and the audience was fantastic. Everything just seemed to line up – the weather, the audience, the vibe and the fact that we were so on. It was like a new chapter. After Download, we went to Nashville to rehearse for the US tour and play at the CMT Awards with Taylor Swift. We were there for a week and some days. We started the American leg of the tour in Camden, New Jersey, on 23 June 2009. The next day, we were off in Cleveland. A small group of us decided to go to the movies. *Transformers 2* was playing. I'm very sure I received a few knowing glances from some of the crew when they realized I would be hanging out with them, since I pretty much always did my own thing. But in all fairness, I wanted to hang out with Helen. I wasn't uncomfortable in the least because my son Rory was also a part of that group. He was working on the tour that summer in the lighting crew. But Helen and I sat away from the rest of the group and pretty much spent the whole movie talking, laughing, telling jokes and getting to know each other, and the weirdest thing happened to me. It was surreal, but when she laughed, I *recognized* her. I can't really describe it except to say that I felt like I knew her, maybe even from another lifetime, but I *knew* her and we shared an intellectual rhythm. I was going to have to tell her.

The next day, I had figured out ahead of time exactly what I was going to say to her and had calculated that I'd need about seven minutes to get it all out. Without hesitation, I broke down my entire personal life. I told her about my live-in girlfriend, my new daughter, my two other children, my ex-wife, and the wife I was still technically married to. I told her I had no clue what her situation was – whether she was married, had kids, was living with someone or what, but I just wanted her to know that I thought we should be together at some point. It could be a year or five years, whatever. I'd wait.

The weirdest thing was that I could tell she was really listening to me, actually taking it all in. There was almost a sense of urgency to get it out. It's funny telling this story now because I remember sharing it with someone else later on who didn't know me very well and that person asked me, 'Well, have you ever been married before or in a serious relationship?' to which I replied, 'I've had more serious relationships in one afternoon than you've probably had in your entire life.' I guess my honesty came over as a sort of naïvety. I was speaking to Helen that way because of the exact opposite. Helen was in her own relationship, which seemed to be as complicated as my confession to her, and which explains why she didn't flinch at my situation. She was boldly upfront about her personal life and in turn told me everything without blinking. Ultimately, we decided then and there to respect each other's space and current relationships.

In reality, my relationship with Shawyana was already coming to an end due to a previous indiscretion on my part. At the same time, Helen's relationship, which had been heavily strained for that past year, completely unravelled for unrelated reasons. During the *Sparkle Lounge* tour we both simultaneously became single and inseparable. So our transition into a full-blown relationship was an easy and natural one. I asked her to marry me on her grand-mother's birthday, 12 August 2009, in Palm Beach, Florida.

The Def Leppard tour continued on until 12 September in Auburn, Washington. Right afterward, Manraze was offered a support slot on the British leg of the Alice Cooper tour in November and December. This was a huge deal for us – Manraze had never done a tour before. Helen had never been to England, so she joined our small 'motley crew' of tech guys to help us. Ronan would do the house sound, Cuz was on drum duty for Paul, and Scotty would do guitars for me and Simon. We would be kind of slum-ming it, as we weren't being paid much, so we didn't feel like splurging on hotels. Simon managed to sort out an amazing deal with a tour bus that had seen better days. But it was totally comfortable, like taking your auntie's front room (complete with the old electric heater) out on tour in wintery Britain. The bus did actually have a portable electric heater, but if you wanted to put the kettle on, you had to unplug the heat; otherwise you'd lose all the power. The tour would hit a lot of the old British theatres that Simon and I had played together thirty years ago in Girl and a few places where Paul and the Sex Pistols had been banned or thrown out. It was magical, playing old stomping grounds. The high point was our show at London's Hammersmith Odeon on 7 December. The next day was my birthday, and we played an intimate show at the Met Bar, a very cool little club in Central London.

After the tour ended, I began travelling to the East Coast to see Helen even while she was working on a production at the John F. Kennedy Center for the Performing Arts. I had rented an apartment in a hip part of DC, so there was much to do. I borrowed a guitar from Brian Meader who worked at a local guitar shop and had lots of time to write new songs for the next Manraze album, *punkfunkrootsrock*, including 'I C U in Everything', which I ended up writing about Helen. While we were there, Helen met my daughter Samantha and Michele. But the most amazing thing came out of Samantha's mouth. She was five at the time. She said to Helen, 'You know, I love my dad very much.' I think it was a protection mechanism. Helen replied, 'Yes. Me too.' And that seemed to be the right answer for Samantha.

In 2010, Def Leppard took a much-needed break. This was the first year we'd taken off since I'd joined in the band. Helen and I got married on 16 July at the Ritz-Carlton in West Palm Beach, Florida. The reason for Florida was because that was where I'd asked her to marry me a year before. However, we recently found out we fucked up on the venue ('*You mean West Palm Beach is different from Palm Beach?*'). I mentioned that I proposed to her on her grandmother's birthday, 12 August. This was because Hattie Simmons, apart from being Helen's grandmother, was also the only mother and father Helen knew. When I began writing this book, Hattie was ninety-five years old, still very sharp and able to share stories about working in the cotton fields of rural North Carolina at the age of five (was that even legal?). Hattie took on the responsibility of raising my wife from birth just as she neared fifty. She worked hard and without breaking just so she could deal with the pressures of raising a child in the sixties and seventies in Brooklyn as a single black woman. Unfortunately, Hattie has since passed away. But we are happy to have had the time we had with her.

I don't like weddings, but this one was great! We had no alcohol, multiple vegetarian food stations (Indian, Mexican,

Thai, soul food, etc.). We then had a second wedding on 12 August, Hattie's ninety-first birthday, at her and Helen's church in Brooklyn. We celebrated Hattie's birthday and had our reception at the same time. We even 'jumped the broom', a time-honoured African-American tradition.

At some point in late 2010, Manraze reconvened in London and talked about what to do next. Our debut album, *Surreal,* had failed to get attention. In 2009, we'd done the Download Festival and the Alice Cooper tour, plus a club tour in 2008 to very empty, cold UK clubs. Paul, Simon and I were brimming with new ideas for a new record, since we really get creative when we're together. I think it's way easier to come up with ideas for Manraze, as there are no restrictions. Someone had said to me that Manraze must satisfy the 'itch that you can't scratch'. That statement is very true when you've been part of a huge band like Def Leppard or the Sex Pistols. Success can sometimes halt your freedom to express yourself creatively because you must continue to fulfil a role. Many great bands have been crucified because they had the audacity to do something different. Bless those that can pull it off. Radiohead said 'Fuck you' and happily went into artistic bliss. However, in their case, Coldplay were waiting in the wings and carried the commercial style baton Radiohead left behind to new stratospheric heights.

Manraze made the album *punkfunkrootsrock* a real

family-and-friends affair. We finished writing the songs fairly quickly, and then it was time to look for a studio on a budget. Simon and Paul cut some live bass and drum tracks at a London studio called Britannia Row, and then Paul called in a favour from Edwyn Collins, who Paul had been playing drums with for years. Ger McDonnell was back in the producer seat. One of Manraze's biggest champions, videographer Mark Sloper, asked if we wanted to do a song for his new docu-movie, *I, Superbiker*. Mark always batted for us before anybody else. He is totally cool and does great work. Mark also accompanies Paul to many Chelsea games. Mark had done documentaries on us previously and had also shot the vid for 'Turn It Up'. After we left Edwyn's studio, we recorded vocals and guitars at Z-Noise studios in Acton, West London, with Robert King, who assisted Ger. While I was recording the lead vocal on 'Closer to Me', Paul and Jeni's daughter, Hollie Cook, a vocalist and recording artist in her own right, started singing harmony in the background. It sounded lovely, so I asked if she'd do it on the record. Hollie is actually a reggae artist, so she fitted right in with our vibe.

Manraze had a great experience doing this album. We recorded everything in eleven days. Helen came up with the album design and took the photos. She also made a video documenting the entire recording process. I remember we shot the pictures for the record with her in a piss-filled alley in Shepherd's Bush, but it still came out looking like a million dollars. We called the album *punkfunkrootsrock* because that's what it was. A mix of punk, funk, roots reggae and rock music that paid tribute to genres we loved and had grown up with.

In the midst of the new Manraze album release, Def Leppard also found ourselves on tour again in 2011. This included another American tour. During one of the tour breaks, Manraze played a show at the famous Roxy in LA to promote *punkfunkrootsrock*. Then it was back on tour with Def Leppard. We headed over to Australia, Japan and New Zealand. Going to New Zealand was great because Helen and I got a chance to spend a few days at our house on the South Island near Queenstown. We ended that year playing a few shows with Mötley Crüe in England. I also found the time to shoot a music video with Mark Sloper at the world-famous Brands Hatch raceway outside London, during the only day it didn't rain, for Manraze's single 'Take on the World', featuring Debbi Blackwell-Cook.

A few years earlier Def Leppard was asked if we wanted to participate in a theatrical rock musical about the eighties called *Rock of Ages*. We passed on the offer because it was in its very early stages and seemed to lack development and finances. Eventually, the play was produced and became a huge success on Broadway, so much so that a movie was to be made based on the show. The movie was to be directed by Adam Shankman, and Tom Cruise would play the lead. The release of the film was to coincide with our 2012 summer US tour, with special guests Poison and Lita Ford, who were also featured in the musical and movie. With this said, it seemed appropriate that we would call our tour Rock of Ages, since it was also the title of our 1983 hit single.

When filming was under way and the band played Florida, we actually paid Tom Cruise a visit on the set, since he'd be singing 'Pour Some Sugar On Me' that day. We wanted to watch him film that segment with the song. When we met him, he told us, 'I'm a little nervous all you guys are here. I learned to sing just for this movie and I really want to give this song the respect it deserves, so go easy on me!' Well, he nailed it. Apparently he trained with a vocal coach for several hours a day to prepare, and it showed. He did lead vocals and backing vocals. I think he did really well, considering he had never sung before.

A few years earlier I had altered my diet slightly by eliminating dairy products. As I evolved mentally and physically and got into better and better shape, it just seemed like the most logical thing to do. Among other research, I had read a book called *The China Study* which had featured heavily in the documentary film *Forks Over Knives*, which advocates a low-fat, plant-based diet as a way to fight disease. It's a brilliant film. Before the movie was over I had decided I would definitely become a vegan. There was no going back for me. In a nutshell, I'd rather feel great than not. And it's not rocket science. Keep active, eat foods that nurture rather than poison your body, and make the effort. That's all I do. It's interesting looking at photos as a timeline. Ross Halfin has been taking photos of me since I was drunk off my ass in the Girl days to the present day.

ROSS HALFIN: After Steve Clark died, Phil cleaned himself up completely. No drinking, no drugs, working out, staying fit and watching what he ate. He even became something strange – a 'vegan'.

Now, you have to put this in the perspective that this was a time when every band was going crazy. Drinking and drugging were the norm, with Phil thinking, *Fuck it. I'm not buying into any of it.* Phil didn't go to rehab – he just stopped. His main focus was staying fit, superfit. A lot of people who make fun of him – Phil's main thing is to be topless within two songs when playing live – are jealous. If I'm shooting Def Leppard, he'll be ready, thinking about what he's wearing, and he knows what looks good. Plus I have to say he's a great poser. And I mean that in a good way.

Prior to kicking off the Rock of Ages tour I got a phone call from my friend Jake Willoughby who had lost his mother to pancreatic cancer. He wasn't really dealing with it all that well, but he wanted to do something special to bring notice to the disease and honour his mother at the same time. Jake had a guitar store and sold my signature guitar model, the Jackson PC1. He asked me if I'd be into auctioning off a customized PC1 for a cancer charity of my choice during the tour.

Just a side note: I've been using Jackson guitars for almost thirty years, and the company has been amazing to me. I often go to the Jackson factory in Corona, California, which is housed within the Fender building. I even hand-splashed more than thirty PC1s for Jackson's thirtieth anniversary, which took months to do but was a lot of messy fun.

So to Jake I said I'd be honoured, since I'd lost my dad to pancreatic cancer, too. However, considering how I feel about the misuse of charitable donations, I didn't want to donate to just any old charity, no matter how glossy the packaging.

As Helen and I checked out a few charities, we were sorely disappointed to find out that in many cases only a fraction of donated dollars goes to the actual suffering party, while the majority of donated dollars gets gobbled up by CEO, staff salaries and write-offs. In fact, legally, a charity only has to give 10 per cent to its particular cause (and even that money still isn't guaranteed to go to the afflicted as long as there is the cost of research to include) and the rest can be frittered away on trips, gifts, hotels, dinners and other varied expenses. Knowing all of this and finding out even more made me very wary about even the most popular of charitable foundations, as they aren't always what they appear to be. In the course of our research, we finally came across the Gerson Institute in San Diego and chose them to be the recipient of the auction's funds.

I first heard of Charlotte Gerson and her father Dr Max Gerson from Jeni Cook, Paul's wife, who is a raw-food chef and gives seminars on juicing and how to incorporate healthy, natural living into the fast-paced lives we lead today. Dr Max Gerson practised medicine until he fled Nazi Germany in 1933 with his family, including his then twelve-year-old daughter Charlotte. He was the grandfather of juicing – extracting the natural vitamins and minerals in liquid form from fruits and vegetables. Nowadays juicing has become very popular, with its obvious health benefits, but back then it was shunned and ridiculed as a medical practice. Dr Gerson had amazing results with 446 out of 450 skin tuberculosis patients using this method. Some of these patients who had cancer also had other illnesses. Gerson managed to reduce their tumours in size with the juice therapy. My fascination with the Gersons didn't stop at Dr Gerson's profound juice therapy practices. His daughter Charlotte persevered through all of the denial and negativity to continue her father's work, which culminated in the Gerson Institute. Her story in itself was inspirational. After more research, Helen and I were absolutely sure we wanted any funds we got for the guitar to go to the Gerson Institute. So after finding all of this out we both made up our minds that we would also like to meet Charlotte Gerson.

Highest bidder and guitar aficionado Murray Bolton from New Zealand won my guitar, which I played all tour, for $20,000. He came by the house in California to pick up the PC1, which had been done up with extraordinary artwork by Mike Learn. Mike included an inscription on the back of the guitar of Jake's mum's and my dad's birth and passing dates. Coincidentally, Jake's mother's name was Connie, same as my mum's.

Then the day arrived. Helen, Debbi (who I had begun singing Motown tunes with around the house and with whom Delta Deep would soon come about); writer Chris Epting, Jake and his wife, Trish, and I went to San Diego to present Charlotte Gerson and the Gerson Institute with the donation. The day was lovely. Press arrived and recorded the entire proceeding, which included a beautiful presentation and a wonderful vegan lunch prepared by the staff. We finally met Charlotte, who was spry and gracious and has more life and energy than a woman a quarter of her age. She had actually healed in record time from a hip fracture and was up and about easily moving around the complex. To say she's healthily energetic is putting it mildly.

I also brought an acoustic guitar so Debbi and I could perform a few songs for everyone. We sang some Motown and blues. I first heard Debbi sing at our wedding. She started singing in the church at the age of two and her voice is kick-ass powerful. Debbi can sing anything. She has sung for a wide range of personalities, from the former Pope John Paul II to Michael Bublé, among many others.

A few interesting things came out of this day. Although my wife had suggested it very early on (I dismissed her idea, as I associate such things with an inflated sense of ego), Chris Epting said, 'Hey, man, you know, you should write a book.' Once again, my immediate reaction was that I didn't like the egotistical element of it. For example, I don't put awards – even the platinum awards – up in our home. I feel weird celebrating my birthday because I already celebrate every day, so what could I possibly do to make one more day even more special? But Chris said, 'No, man, it's a really interesting life and different from [those of] your peers.' The other occurrence that pushed yet another chapter of my life into full throttle was everyone's enquiries about where to purchase songs by Debbi and me. Delta Deep was on its way.

Helen, Debbi and I soon left for New Zealand to spend time at our house there. Soon after arriving, we heard a Wilson Pickett song on the radio in a store. We started commenting on the vibe and groove of the song. The conversation continued when we got back to the house. That inspiration turned into the song 'Miss Me', which took on its own identity. When we returned to the States, the three of us continued writing songs together. Helen dubbed the band Delta Deep. For some reason, in the music business, it's always considered taboo to write music with your wife. I think that stems from male-based sexist views, misogyny and insecurity. Suffice to say, we flow really naturally together, one of the beautiful benefits of intellectual rhythm. It was also really cool to see Debbi just oozing out melodies and lyrics, too. It's amazing what happens when you're inspired and have great chemistry with people.

Next we started recording a version of the Tina Turner song 'Black Coffee', which was made famous by Stevie Marriott and Humble Pie. Ironically, during this time Paul and Jeni Cook were staying at our house in Cali for a bit of a holiday, so I asked Paul if he'd play drums on it. He loved the Humble Pie version and had just seen it on YouTube the previous week. Once Paul cut his drums, it was obvious Simon had to play bass on the song, giving it a London/USA groove (featuring Manraze), just like Marriott's version. Then some weird shit happened.

In the spring of 2013, Def Leppard was booked to play a residency in Las Vegas. I was never really into doing a residency in Vegas. I always associated that with the mob and casinos in the desert where the Rat Pack performed. When we first played there in 1983, we performed at the Aladdin Theater for the Performing Arts, and Paul Anka was doing a residency. Vegas was never really associated with hard-rock bands. But how things have changed, and with eleven shows to be played at the Joint in the Hard Rock Hotel and Casino, it would be a first for Def Leppard to perform that many times in one city. So after thirty years, here we were, doing something brand new.

As was becoming the trend, we were asked if we would play the *Hysteria* album in full. Fans were growing accustomed to having that full-album experience recreated for them, and we loved the idea. In fact, Joe and I had actually been talking about doing this very same thing for about twenty years. Now we finally would get to fulfil that ambition. To me, *Hysteria* is the definitive Def Leppard album.

The shows in Vegas were being dubbed *Viva Hysteria*. The whole thing turned into something bigger than we ever would have imagined, as it would be filmed and recorded for a movie, DVD, CD and potential documentary. We agreed that if we were going to do this, we had to do it right. We wanted to make it very different to anything we had ever done before. We knew that the *Hysteria* set would be an hour long, but we wanted to give the audience much more than that. We decided to also be our own opening act, playing rare songs and deep cuts. And we decided to give this act another name, to set it off from the rest of the show. We named ourselves Ded Flatbird, a name which has a pretty amusing genesis. When my son Rory's mum, Jacki, was in Lamaze class back in 1989, one of the other mothers-to-be asked Jacki what her husband did. Jacki replied, 'He's in a band called Def Leppard.' The woman repeated back, 'Ded Flatbird?' It was a story that became a favourite within the Leppard circle, so much so that our manager,

Peter Mensch, had T-shirts printed up. And so the legendary moniker was born.

The plan was to make the raw opening set forty-five minutes. But before the first show, during our production rehearsals a couple of weeks earlier in Los Angeles, there was something different. Rick Allen was practising 'Good Morning Freedom' (a B-side from the first album that would also be our first live song of the evening) when he stopped playing and said, 'Wow. The last time I played this song I had two arms, so I need a minute to think about how I'm going to approach this.' That gave me pause. In the nearly thirty years since the accident, Rick remained an amazing inspiration for millions of people all around the world and especially for us, his bandmates. He's adapted so incredibly to his injury that it's easy for us to sometimes forget that he has a disability. When he made the remark about 'Good Morning Freedom', it reminded me that no matter how easy he may make it look, at the end of the day Rick grew up playing a lot of these songs with both of his arms. Subsequently, during the same rehearsals, Viv revealed some disturbing news. He had been diagnosed with Hodgkin's lymphoma. What we all thought was a lingering cough turned out to be cancer. Viv performed in Vegas, but immediately afterward, he began aggressive treatment.

The shows we played during our stay in Las Vegas were some of the most powerful and energetic we'd ever played. Part of it was that we knew Viv was ill and so we had to push things a little bit more. We filled in the gaps and made it work. The intimacy of the venue certainly helped fuel the excitement and intensity of the shows. But I think the biggest difference was in the fact that all of the guys were feeling that this residency might be perceived as some sort of victory lap, and so we all pushed back collectively and as ferociously as we could. We showed everyone we were still hungry, tenacious and committed to raising the bar. For the VIPs, we did something we had never done before – a meet-and-greet, plus an exclusive acoustic performance before the main show. I couldn't believe the scene – fans from all over the world, fans breaking down and crying as we played the acoustic set, fans who had seen us as many as forty times. The *Viva Hysteria* experience in Las Vegas was so powerful and so positive that any thought I had that this band was winding down was pretty much eliminated. In fact, due to the show's success, we were asked to do a tour of European festivals during the summer of 2013, earning one of the biggest paydays we'd ever had.

But it was right before we were due to set off on that European tour that I had my hand injury. The tendon tore off the bone of one of my left knuckles. I couldn't play guitar properly and would need surgery. Still, the tour started in two days and I got through it all. When the tour was done, I went to Paris and had my surgery done by a brilliant hand surgeon named Jean-Noël Goubier. He sews fingers back onto people's hands for a living, so I was definitely in good hands, so to speak. After the surgery, I had to wear a cast on my wrist and arm for six weeks, which left me with a withered, atrophied non-guitar-playing wrist and hand when the cast came off. My physical therapist Scott Moncrief was amazing as well. He helped me strengthen my wrist and fingers over several months. Since my need for expression never goes away, and knowing I couldn't play guitar as I normally do, I entered an interim period for a few months where I would still (at the very least) be able to express myself.

I had never played slide guitar before, but as I couldn't press down on the strings, I thought this would be as good a time as any to learn. I literally pulled up a ten-minute tutorial video on YouTube by Joe Walsh, and a week later I recorded the song 'Bang the Lid', which is all slide and my official debut bottleneckin' it. Deb, Helen and I (as Delta Deep) wrote the song about a female slave killing her slave owner with sex. I could never write a song like that by my 'white self', but with a sultry sixty-two-year-old black woman and an aware soul sistah from Brooklyn, when it came to going in deep and dark, it was game on, no boundaries. We would also cover other 'elephant in the room' taboo subjects like we did in 'Down in the Delta', which is about being uprooted from your home country, seeing your entire family killed and then being forced into a burning living hell on earth as a slave in a new land with no chance of escape. All of a sudden these songs weren't standard blues. They had fire, passion, a fuck-offness, and an unholy groove I hadn't heard anywhere before. We've been calling it alternative roots, extreme blues, blues rock 'n' soul, but actually, it's a hybrid of all the above, as, through Debbi's vocals, it channels the pain and suffering ever-present in the lives of real blues artists from a century ago.

In a perpetual moving-forward motion, I bumped into the phenomenal drummer Forrest Robinson at Rick Allen's fiftieth birthday party in Malibu. Rick and I had met Forrest when he played drums for India.Arie more than ten years ago. We were standing in the wings watching the show and we said, 'Fuck! Who's this guy on drums?!' After we met Forrest, he told us that all he really wanted to do was rock out and that just because he was a black man with dreads (my friend Rudi Riviere faces the same dilemma when it comes to being viewed as a credible rocker), it didn't mean he couldn't rock with the best of them. Forrest is of a rare pedigree. He was a heavy metal drummer (plays the fastest double-kick bass drum I've ever heard) with soul roots who played for Joe Sample and the Crusaders. He impressively filled the shoes of Steve Gadd. At the party that night, when I played him the demo for 'Miss Me', he was floored and wanted in on the band.

The next piece of this puzzle was laid in place once again by Chris Epting. 'Hey, man, have you ever met Robert DeLeo from the Stone Temple Pilots? You'd really like him and he'd be perfect on this.' Again, don't judge a book by its cover. Aside from him and his brother Dean being songwriting geniuses who propelled Stone Temple Pilots to star status in the nineties, Robert is also a disciple of Motown bass legend James Jamerson and loves James Brown and holy funk. When Forrest and Robert played with me and Debbi, it all went so far in a different, amazing direction until all of a sudden the music sounded like Aretha Franklin was singing with Led Zeppelin. It was at that point that Delta Deep was truly born.

The year 2014 brought on a double headlining tour with KISS. It was one of the most fulfilling tours we've ever done. This was the most extremely positive case of two bands *not* competing for centre stage but pooling all of their resources together, crew included, to put on the most spectacular live event of the summer. Egos were willingly checked at the door. Both bands circled the wagons and it was us against the world. Many people asked, 'What are the KISS guys like?', 'Are they egocentric?' to which I replied, 'They are all faithful disciples of their own band, KISS.' The fact that Paul Stanley, Gene Simmons, Eric Singer and Tommy Thayer will sometimes take three hours to prepare for a show so that their fans are not disappointed speaks volumes and puts them way above any other rock band I've ever known, not to mention Paul and Gene are doing this into their sixty-plus years of age.

The tour was a raging success and put us into a really good state for the 2015 tour, on which we had to contend with a few issues. One of these was that Viv's cancer had returned, so he had to receive treatment for the first few dates of the US leg. An old friend of mine, Steve Brown from Trixter, filled in for Viv with his awesome guitar and vocal talents. On a great note, the dates were selling like hotcakes. Since I'm writing this section at the start of that tour, I'll let you know how it goes, considering the Def Leppard self-titled album won't be released until about the same time this book comes out.

About that album: we initially went in to record an EP or a single, as albums are fairly out of vogue these days. But twelve songs flowed out. From that point on, we worked each song as though it was its own separate project. It was a bit like in the old days where Zeppelin, Bowie or the Stones would write a few songs, go in and record the material while they were still hot on it. We were in Dublin three times recording in this fashion – January 2014, May 2014 and January 2015. We did this even with a tour in between. One of the main reasons I think we recorded like this was that we were doing this album for us. We didn't have to appease a record executive, a label or fans. I feel like that's true artistic expression. You're not doing it for financial reasons or for special kudos. It's just solid artistic integrity, where fulfilment is the reward.

Over the last few years, I've realized why I started playing guitar. It wasn't because I wanted to be a great guitar player: it was because I wanted to get something out, like scratching an itch. There are lots of elements of guitar playing that I'm not even remotely interested in. The guitar was my choice as a tool of expression. It's the same as when I write lyrics or finish recording a song where there's not necessarily a guitar in it. It's the relief of creative release. Yes. I know that sounds a bit rude.

In 1994, although we started recording the *Slang* album with a different process than that of earlier albums – *Adrenalize*, *Hysteria* – I don't think we got the full memo. As much as I enjoyed the recording process and the way it sounded, it wasn't quite finished off. We could have made the songs better with just a little bit more work. We only wanted to write the songs, record them and be done. In hindsight, if we had actually reflected on the *Slang* songs like we did on this new album, I think they would have been superior. I feel that with this new album we finally hit on what we all think is a successful way to record Def Leppard.

With everything I've done and all the music I've made, including with Def Leppard, I have never received more immediate praise for my guitar playing and singing than I have with Delta Deep. I think the reasons for this include the fact that the whole project is such an output of raw emotions and very much in line with true blues artists. The question that keeps coming up is, 'Why do you play and sing completely different on this album than you do on the Def Leppard stuff?' to which my answer is, 'I play the same guitars and I play the same style. It's just the context that's different.'

In Def Leppard, we create a structure that houses guitar themes, melodies, massive counter vocal harmonies with counter rhythm harmonies so there's no real space for one-take improvisation. Def Leppard sets sonic rules that our songs have to abide by. In Delta Deep, there's an organic flow that just instantly oozes out and you have to let it. My role is the same in both bands but yields different sounds, given the disparate contexts.

And then there's the feeling. Helen, Debbi and I write together. Some of those songs are influenced by painful realities in Helen's and Debbi's lives like the fact that Helen has lost two of her three brothers to gun-related murder and Debbi lost her youngest son in the same way. These elements as well as others influence the outpouring of emotions that you hear in these songs. The unexpected, overwhelmingly positive response to our self-titled debut album *Delta Deep*, which came out on 23 June 2015, was equalled only by the response to our first show that we played together at the Hotel Cafe in Hollywood. All of the influences (James Brown, Led Zeppelin, Aretha Franklin, the Stones, Sly and the Family Stone, B. B. King, Billie Holiday), surprisingly to us, made an appearance onstage. I am loving this whole experience as I'm loving the new Def Leppard album and tour, although they are two polar opposite events. As my experiences multiply, the need to express myself also increases. I'm in awe of the avenues that continually present themselves that allow me to do so.

# Coda

I am going to end this book on a note about who I am and what I am in tune with as a person, as opposed to the perception of who I am as a rock musician. My great friend Rudi Riviere and I often confer and concur about life in general. We both came from the East End of London and have had successes in our own rights. We often remark about how neither of us has even slightly changed from when we first met. But our circumstances and many of the people around us have completely changed. This causes us both to have a very keen sense of observation and appreciation. For instance, the fantasy and excitement of meeting famous people when one is in a travelling rock band is extremely overrated. The most noteworthy moments in my life are not always the ones people think they will be (i.e. meeting other rock stars, being on tour, attending after-show gatherings). Instead it's the times in my life when I am blessed to share experiences with those whose lives and mental capacities have been put to the ultimate test. It's these moments that keep my life interesting and me interested in my life. In fact, some of the most interesting people I have met and learned from are people you would never have heard of. Immaculée Ilibagiza is one of those people.

Immaculée Ilibagiza beat the odds big-time and I met her. She is a native Rwandan Tutsi, and her story happened at the peak of her country's most violent period, where one million Rwandans – which constituted about 20 per cent of the country's population – were killed. Her entire family was slain while she hid in the bathroom of a compassionate Hutu pastor's house with seven other women for ninety-one days as her tormentors called her name on the other side of the wall saying they would chop her up with their machetes.

One day Helen and I received a text from Immaculée saying she would be speaking in the area. We drove to meet her and we all went out for dinner. It was amazing to meet such a woman who had gone through so much and yet was so willing to talk about every detail. Both Helen and I each had copies of her book, *Left to Tell: Discovering God Amidst the Rwandan Holocaust*, which we read in its entirety. We sat at the restaurant long after our meal was over asking questions about those painful moments. Immaculée encouraged our curiosity and answered every question with such wisdom and insight. It was truly an amazing opportunity to get to meet her. She calls us her brother and sister, and I couldn't think of better titles. Immaculée accepted her fate so graciously and humbly. Yet there are people who deal with far less and stumble at the first hurdle. It was such a pleasure for us to be in the company of someone who had encountered the world's evils face-to-face but had managed to emerge smiling and with open arms and forgiveness. Meeting someone like that has a way more profound effect on me than if I meet another celebrity.

Now, I'm sure many of you are wondering about or may even be appalled by my ability to be more philosophical about the perils of life than about a barre chord. In my travels, people have often asked me what the coolest thing about being a rock star is, fully expecting a totally shallow anecdote or a proud possession as an answer. But I always answer, 'Having access to the study of human nature and its psychology.' It's a bit like when Robin Williams's character in the seventies sitcom *Mork & Mindy* reports to his extra-terrestrial superior about what he'd learned on earth that particular week. It never fails to fascinate me to connect the dots between social interaction, world history, relationships, human greed, politics, and human beings being biological animals with potential – however limited – access to spiritual enlightenment. At no time has this been more apparent than right now, in the 'me, me, me' culture of today's connection to social media and obsession with every version of celebrity.

I am totally aware that the industry I am in contributes

to the 'dumbing down' of the world. In fact, it's a premier tool. But as with everything else, once you get further down the rabbit hole, the real truth becomes more apparent. The epic task of numbing and dumbing a whole generation results in some interesting outcomes, whether it be public tears of sadness from a celebrity over another celeb's romantic break-up broadcast live at an awards show the same week that Steven Sotloff was publicly decapitated by ISIS on internet video (yielding not even a concerned sigh from the celebrity elite); or the public's over-the-top publicized and advertised desire to feed the less fortunate on Thanksgiving Day, ironically just one week after a ninety-two-year-old former Second World War veteran was arrested for trying to feed the homeless in Florida. However, we don't seem to have a problem letting the less fortunate feed and fend for themselves for the remaining 364 days of the year. You can't help but think that the reasons for this outpouring of kindness to other humans for such a short span of time is being done for reasons that will somehow benefit someone's self-image. I think it's called reciprocal altruism, where an organism will do something for another organism to its own detriment, expecting a reward for the deed later. In a nutshell, what I'm trying to say, based on my experience, is that no one actually cares. This is nothing new. But the fact that I strut around onstage half-naked for half the year doesn't mean that I'm not aware of other life-changing events all around me.

We humans have always been really self-absorbed, as evidenced by the hedonistic habits of the Roman Empire elite, the gross practice of enslavement that resulted in more than a hundred million African slaves dying at the hands of their captors, and ethnic cleansing from today all the way to further back than we can record. In fact, this last practice never seems to run out of steam, having taken the shape of the slaughter of Native Americans at the hands of European invaders, eventually called 'settlers', the extermination of Jews in Nazi Germany, the Indonesian occupation of East Timor, and the Bosnian genocide in Bosnia and Herzegovina (formerly part of Yugoslavia). So it's interesting that human nature hasn't actually changed much throughout the centuries. We've just found convenient ways to convince ourselves that we're living in a civilized world where the occasional bad seed ruins it for everyone. But really, there is always confirmation of grotesque evidence of human cruelty.

I've found that the travelling part of being a rock star is the most valuable if you can be receptive and open-minded. I would never have found myself deep in conversation with extreme intellectuals in India or talking politics in Moscow with a Russian dissident or speaking with the Queen of England had I never left the burglar alarm factory in Walthamstow. I found myself inside the octagon training ring while UFC light heavyweight world champion Jon Jones prepared for his 2012 UFC title defense fight against Vitor Belfort at Greg Jackson's awesome training camp in

New Mexico. I also attended, at the BAM Fisher rehearsal studio in Brooklyn, the Urban Bush Women's dance company preparation for their tribute to John Coltrane's *A Love Supreme.* I've found that with every one of these experiences, I see a common thread or pattern emerging in human nature. If I had not had all of these experiences and had not taken something useful away for myself, I would have thought it all random. But if you look back at history, you'll see the reasoning behind all events, be it an empire protecting its monarchy, or so-called leaders or governments desperately protecting the profits of an elite class or its corporations above all else. As this pattern lays itself out, you can also look at your own personal history and see a correlation to almost everything you've experienced as a kind of cosmic map. Although it sucks and seems hopeless, I'd rather know than not know. There is something almost joyous about this path to self-discovery because it all makes sense on a certain level.

A lot of people ask me who my favourite icon or idol is in history. Apart from the obvious, with Jimi Hendrix being a pioneer of hybrid musical styles or Bruce Lee regarding martial arts, I love the fact that Mahatma Gandhi stood up to the British Empire in a pair of flip-flops and liberated India in a peaceful fashion. This unfortunately would later get him killed, proving my point about civilization's amorality. The world is spinning on its axis in corruption as we try our best to reverse its direction. Not going to happen.

We are steeped in denial and awash in hope. Either way, the world is winning. From drugs to technology, we are inundated with the latest and greatest to keep us docile. The most ravenous out-of-control junkies are the ones who practise their addiction within the legal loopholes of prescription drugs supplied by the most powerful cartel on earth. The dice are loaded and the game is totally rigged. It's nothing new, though – it's how every empire gets to be an empire. Mass control is easy. Religion, alcohol, sports, entertainment (my industry), radio, the internet and TV – reality or otherwise – totally take everybody's eye off the ball. You only have to look out of a window anywhere to see the latest incarnation of the obedient consumer completely zombie-ing out on the smartphone to know all is lost (and although I have had my own episodes of zombification, I'm writing this chapter the old-fashioned way, with a pen and paper, in London on Mother's Day, by the way). What's really scary is that if you did let the public take control, it'd probably be way worse. But that's the plan, right? It'd be the lunatics taking over the asylum and all that'd really happen is that they would have their credibility, integrity and all their good senses taken away from them.

There are obviously some superbright caring people out there who don't just have business interests as their main objective. But they either have no voice or they also have a price. So the more things change, the more they stay the same. The power remains truly entrenched with the powerful. You just need to look at any country in history to see that the plan and the outcome always end up the same. Growth. Peak. Control. Domination. Violent demise.

And then there's the violence. Many people are not responsible enough to be in control of a conversation or a car, let alone a semiautomatic assault rifle. The majority of the public doesn't fall into the category of the civilized few. If they did, then everyone could walk around with a gun and there would never be a problem. Two of the most violent world history events, and an elephant in the room – the 1945 atomic bombing of Hiroshima and Nagasaki is really only the tip of the iceberg. I actually went to a Hiroshima memorial where a portion of the bombed area was left as ground zero. There were pictures of children with their flesh melted off and even a slab of ground onto which is burned the shadow of a body, disintegrated in the blast. There's always a constant flow of violence in society. If we're lucky enough to live in the ivory towers (which we call 'hubs of civilization' around the world), we like to kid ourselves that things are actually getting better. It's my assessment that we're way off the mark and that atrocity and animalistic behaviour are the norm. Only a few are truly civilized, and that has nothing to do with race, creed, religion or anything. On that note, it took me fifty-one years and meeting millions of people to realize that the person who most closely resembled me in all aspects of myself on this planet was of opposite gender, from a different country than me, and of another race – my wife, Helen. My point being, you can't generalize when you talk about countries, races and 'types'. It actually comes down to the individual.

As for religion (I know, I know. Never talk about religion. *Who made that rule anyway?*), don't fear God. Fear the devil. Ironically, it seems most people worship the devil, thinking he's God, but God should be about love, right? I definitely notice there's not a lot of love around, and that's the problem. I could never really understand why someone would proclaim to be a devout Christian and break the hallowed rule of Christianity and go and kill innocent animals for fun or pleasure. If you're starving and you're eating that animal for survival, that's one thing but torturing one of God's creatures and making it suffer in death for your ego's enjoyment is yet another sin, if I'm not mistaken. As we get older and, I like to believe, more experienced, we ask ourselves questions that we wouldn't have even heard before because we were buzzing around being totally distracted. The question is usually, 'Is there a greater power?' or 'Is Darwinian theory the way to go?' I like to think there's an answer that's ethereal and clean but the best way I've heard it described is that there's an energy source linked to a collective conscience.

I've personally followed an Eastern philosophy called Sant Mat for about twenty-five years that goes along with this train of thought. But then again, who knows what's out there? I'm not freaked out about dying – in fact, I welcome it. As I tell my daughter Samantha, 'Dying is as natural as being born, and we have to do both, so don't sweat it.' I also think this level of humanity and acceptance of the inevitable is the way it's supposed to be. The only escape is via some spiritual enlightenment, which is the soul's equivalent to Captain Kirk's 'Beam me up, Scotty' ideology. I always view this place as the earth plane, one rung up from hell. That all makes sense spiritually, but so does 'You die, you're dead, and that's it.' With our biggest enemy being our minds, our egos can make us see and believe things that aren't actually there. We are the masters of our own illusions. So the bottom line is that we each have to take our own path. We are all 'works in progress', different stations on the same train line.

In closing, I'd like to say that I hope I am way further up the line than I was when I started experiencing this earth plane almost fifty-eight years ago. Although I've got a way to go, I have inherited some amazing philosophies and experiences along the way, onstage and off. If I can manifest them positively before I die and show that the lessons actually stuck, then and only then will my microscopic pinpoint of existence in this universe have really mattered.

# Picture Acknowledgements

All images are supplied courtesy of the author unless otherwise stated. Any copyright holders who have been overlooked are invited to get in touch with the publisher.

Photos 26, 32, 55: Ross Halfin
Photo 28: Denis O'Regan
Photo 43: Mike Steele Photography
Photo 45, 54: Kerika Fields Photos
Photos 46–51, 53, 56: Helen L. Collen

# Index

## About the Authors

**Phil Collen** is the lead guitarist of the legendary rock band Def Leppard. He has been a vegetarian for 31 years, alcohol-free for 28 years, and vegan for over four years, busting the myth of the classic rock star stereotype.

**Chris Epting** is the author of many books, including *Led Zeppelin Crashed Here*, *All I Really Need to Know I Learned from KISS*, and *Hello, It's Me, Dispatches From a Pop Culture Junkie*.